Heidegger and the Question of Time

Heidegger and the Question of Time

—◆—

Françoise Dastur

Translated by
François Raffoul
and David Pettigrew

Humanity
Books

an imprint of Prometheus Books
59 John Glenn Drive, Amherst, New York 14228-2197

Published 1999 by Humanity Books, an imprint of Prometheus Books

Inquiries should be addressed to
Humanity Books, 59 John Glenn Drive, Amherst, New York 14228–2197.
VOICE: 716–691–0133, ext. 207. FAX: 716–564–2711.

Originally published in French as *Heidegger et la Question du Temps*
by Presses Universitaires de France in 1990.

© Presses Universitaires de France, 1990
12, rue Jean-de Beauvais, 75005 Paris, France

03 02 01 00 99   6 5 4 3 2

Library of Congress Cataloging-in-Publication Data

Dastur, Françoise, 1942–
　　[Heidegger et la question du temps. English]
　　Heidegger and the question of time / Françoise Dastur ; translated by François Raffoul and David Pettigrew.
　　　　p.　　cm. — (Contemporary studies in philosophy and the human sciences)
　　Includes bibliographical references and index.
　　ISBN 1–57392–395–8
　　1. Heidegger, Martin, 1889–1976—Contributions in philosophy of time.
2. Time—History—20th century. I. Title. II. Series.
B3279.H49D33　　1997
115′.092—dc21　　　　　　　　　　　　　　　　96–40852
　　　　　　　　　　　　　　　　　　　　　　　　　CIP

Contents

—◆—

Abbreviations

——◆——

ER: *The Essence of Reasons* (Evanston: Northwestern University Press, 1969).

H: *Heraclitus Seminar, 1966–1967* (University: Alabama University Press, 1979).

HCT: *History of the Concept of Time: Prolegomena* (Bloomington: Indiana University Press, 1985).

HPT: Preface to William J. Richardson's *Heidegger: Through Phenomenology to Thought* (The Hague: Martinus Nijhoff, 1967).

ID: *Identity and Difference* (New York: Harper & Row, 1969).

IM: *An Introduction to Metaphysics* (Garden City, NY: Doubleday-Anchor Books, 1961).

KPM: *Kant and the Problem of Metaphysics* (Bloomington: Indiana University Press, 1990).

MFL: *Metaphysical Foundations of Logic* (Bloomington: Indiana University Press, 1984).

OWL: *On The Way to Language* (New York: Harper & Row, 1971).

PLT: *Poetry, Language, Thought* (New York: Harper & Row, 1971).

PR: *The Principle of Reason* (Bloomington: Indiana University Press, 1991).

PT: "Principles of Thinking," in *The Piety of Thinking* (Bloomington: Indiana University Press, 1976).

QCT: *The Question Concerning Technology and Other Essays* (New York: Harper and Row, 1977).

QIV: *Questions IV* (Paris: Gallimard, 1976).

RA: *The Rectorate Address*, in "The Self-Assertion of the German University", Review of Metaphysics, 38 (1985).

TB: *On Time and Being* (New York: Harper & Row, 1972).

WCT: *What is Called Thinking?* (New York: Harper & Row, 1968).

WP: *What is Philosophy?* (New Haven, CT: College & University Press, 1958).

Translators' Preface

———◆———

The author of this remarkable little book has enjoyed the admiration of her students at the Sorbonne, where she has been teaching since 1971, as well as the esteem of her colleagues. Françoise Dastur's teaching bears essentially on the German philosophical tradition, Kantian and post-Kantian, with a special emphasis on phenomenology, in which she is a renowned specialist. Her works on Husserl, Merleau-Ponty, Heidegger, and more broadly on the phenomenological movement as a whole are numerous. For the last several years, Dastur's reflection has focused particularly on the question of time, on its relation to language and to finitude. This research led to the publication, recently, of her *thèse d'état*, "Bringing Time into Language: An Attempt at a Phenomenological Chrono-logy" ("Dire le Temps: Esquisse d'une chrono-logie phénoménologique), a subtitle that borrows an expression from Heidegger's 1925–26 course (GA 21, pp. 199–200), which Dastur translated into French. The central question, or enigma, that guides Dastur's work is the possibility of bringing presence into language, or, more accurately, of bringing the very *event* of presence into language. What language, what grammar, and what syntax could name the sheer event of coming into Being, the temporal bursting forth of Being? In Dastur's words: How can one bring into language the "*advent* in its pure nakedness, not the advent of some thing or some one, but the advent *itself* and its *concealed event?*"[1]

Nowhere has this verbal, active, in a word, *temporal,* sense of presence been thought as radically as in Martin Heidegger's work, thanks to a phenomenological "destruction" of the traditional mode of *substantiality.* The destruction of this latter sense opens the possibility to think together Being and time, to understand Being *as* time. Françoise Dastur has explored this identity between time and being in a meditation on death and finitude,[2] through a reflection on the tragic in Hölderlin,[3] on time and language in her *thèse d'état,* and in this essay on the question of temporality in Heidegger's work. According to Dastur, the essential contribution of Heidegger's ontological inquiry is to bring out the *temporal* meaning of Being. As she makes clear from the very beginning of her essay, "the whole originality of Heidegger's thought turns on the clarification of the *Temporal* meaning of what the Western tradition from its inception (Parmenides, Plato, and Aristotle) has called 'Being.' "[4]

This work is distinctive in at least two respects. First, because the problematic of temporality in Heidegger's thinking is presented and analyzed in its thematic unity for the first time, a surprising fact considering that, as Dastur herself notes, the problem of the relation between Being and time is "the 'center' of Heidegger's 'philosophy'" (HQT, xxii). Second, because it embraces, with a rare lucidity and rigor, the entirety of Heidegger's work on this issue, from his 1916 habilitation thesis, *The Theory of Categories and Signification in Duns Scotus*, until his last seminars, Thor and Zähringen, by way of the major stages of *Being and Time*, of fundamental ontology, and of the historical meditation on the epochality of Being. One of the most impressive achievements of this book is to have brought together a wide range of writings from Heidegger on the question of time, and to have discerned their inner connection. Dastur retraces here a complex and often enigmatic "path of thinking," at once revolutionary and yet meditative, by following the thread of a constantly renewed reflection on Being and time, on Being *as* time, on the enigma of the "and" in Being *and* time.

1. THE SITE OF THE QUESTION OF TIME

Françoise Dastur's stated intention is simple. What is at issue is to think philosophically—that is, far from the petty polemics and other political-academic-ideological battles—what Heidegger never ceased to consider as the *central* question of his thought: the co-belonging of Being and time. This co-belonging of Being and time, that is, the fact that Being itself must be thought *as* time, is emphasized in the writings of the young Heidegger by the use of a specific term to designate the Temporality of Being itself, *Temporalität*, in contrast with the more common term, *Zeitlichkeit*, which Heidegger uses to designate the temporality of the human Dasein. Dastur insists on this fundamental distinction between *Zeitlichkeit*—which we render by "temporality" with a lowercase letter—and *Temporalität*, which we render by an upper-case letter, thus using the same term for both designations (HQT, 74). For, if the question of time is approached in *Being and Time* on the basis of the temporality of a particular entity—Dasein—the central issue of the inquiry nevertheless is to bring to light the Temporality of Being itself, on the basis of a deconstruction (*Destruktion*) of the traditional identification between Being and presence. This implies a twofold gesture: 1) the rejection of the way in which Being, in the tradition, has been dissociated from time and identified with eternity; 2) the removal of time from the domain of entities, whether the physical entity or the psychical entity, to which it has been confined in the tradition. As Heidegger explains in paragraph 5 of *Being and Time*, time has always served as an "ontological—*or rather ontical*—criterion for naively discriminating various realms of entities" (BT, 18/39, our emphasis). But time is here instead conceived of as the horizon of the understanding of *Being* itself. This resolutely ontological orientation allows Heidegger to understand the entire philosophical tradition as a "vulgar," that is, an ontic, interpretation of time: the opposition no longer lies between time and eternity, physical time and psychological time, inner sense and outer sense, duration and spatialized time; all these distinctions are *ontical* in the sense that they do not problematize the Temporal sense of Being itself. The issue is no longer to understand how time can structure different regions of entities (nature, history, etc.), but rather how it can be the horizon for an understanding of *Being*. Dastur shows that Heidegger's entire thought with respect to time resides in this meditation on the intimate relation of time and Being. "The question of Being and the question of time therefore do not represent two separate themes of Heidegger's thought: the 'novelty' of *Being and Time*, on the contrary, consists precisely in having made of these two traditional problems a *single* question, that of the Temporality of Being" (HQT, 9). As Heidegger stated in a passage from the 1930 course, *On the Essence of Human Freedom*: "We do not question Being alone, and we do not question time alone either. Neither do we question Being and also time; rather we question their *inner co-belonging* and what springs from it" (GA 31, 118). Being is to be thought on the basis of time: such is the meaning of the reappropriation of the concept of presence, which is referred to its temporal origin as *ousia*, constant presence in the present; furthermore, time is no longer that "lesser" being of which Aristotle spoke at the beginning of chapter 10 of Book IV of his *Physics*, but Being itself in its very givenness and eventfulness. Being: something temporal, Temporal; time: something which has the character of Being. This circle of Being and time will represent the core of the meditation that we find in the 1962 lecture "Time and Being." Being is no longer simply what is present, but rather presence itself, in its movement and its manifestation; and time is no longer confined to the order of entities but is involved in the event of presence.

However, this site of the co-belonging of time and Being can be accessed only through a phenomenological destruction of the traditional conceptions of time. All of the traditional problematics with respect to time—antinomies between physical time and psychical time, time of the subject and the time of the world, aporias of the existence of time, problems of the spatial representation of time, the representation of time as a succession of nows—must be rejected at the threshold of this meditation on time and Being. This critical distance with respect to the tradition is manifest in the early writings of the young Heidegger on time in historical science. Dastur recalls how Heidegger, in terms that are very similar to those of Bergson, establishes a difference between measurable, objective, homogeneous time, that is, quantified time, and qualitative time, which is proper to historical time. This first critique of scientific time is developed in the famous lecture of July 1924, "The Concept of Time." A decisive step was taken there, for it was not only a question of delineating in a critical way the proper field of objective time, but also of noting positively that time intrinsically involves "human life" in its individual character, which Heidegger already names Dasein. Time does not answer to the question "What is time?" but rather "Who is time?"

Certainly, at least since St. Augustine, and perhaps in a sense since Aristotle, the link between time and the "soul" was established. Time as numbering number seems to implicate the psyche (Aristotle); time is a "distention of the soul" (Augustine); time is the form of inner sense (Kant); finally, with Husserl, the analysis of time takes place within the context of "internal-time consciousness." But Dastur insists on the fact that Heidegger gives a radical formulation to this unity between time and subjectivity, a unity that had remained insufficiently developed by the tradition. Indeed, it is not sufficient to posit, as Kant did, the juxtaposition of time and the "I think"; and it is not sufficient either to characterize time as inner sense, thus leaving a problematic "outside realm." As Dastur puts it, "the virtue of the Heideggerian problematic, instead, is that it negates the very subject-object distinction" (HQT, xxx). The task is thus both to posit the *identity* of time and of the "subject" and to destroy the subjectivist conception of the subject. According to Dastur, it is this twofold task that defines the elaboration of the concept of Dasein, an elaboration which, according to Heidegger in the 1928 summer semester course, would amount to nothing less than to "revolutionize the whole concept of the human being" (MFL, 133/167).

This revolution thus begins with the destruction of the subject-object opposition. Time is no longer subjective time nor time of the soul, but the "first-name" (*Vor-name*) of Being itself. Dastur stresses this inaugural break with the subjectivist (and in particular Husserlian) problematic of time. Heidegger's question "was determined on the basis of the question of Being: on the basis of the question of *Being* and precisely not on the basis of a reflection on *consciousness* and its internal temporality. This is why he emphasized that his question was foreign to Husserl's problematics of an internal consciousness of time" (HQT, 8). Nevertheless, at the time of *Sein und Zeit* Being is only *accessible* on the basis of a certain questionableness (*Fraglichkeit*), which is situated in a particular entity, Dasein, that is, the entity who I am each time; consequently, in order to bring out the Temporal character of Being, it will be necessary to go through an ontological analysis of Dasein.

Such an analysis, Dastur stresses, aims at exhibiting the fundamental structures of existence, or *existentialia*. The clarification of the temporal structure of Dasein thus implies the analysis of these existentialia. Dastur distinguishes three essential stages in this elucidation of the temporality of Dasein in *Being and Time*, an elucidation which itself, she insists, is only a preliminary stage on the way toward an elaboration of the question of the co-belonging of Being and time. 1) The analysis of the basic items of *everyday* existence. As Dastur explains, it is "the *factical* existence of Dasein that needs to be analyzed, without starting from a presupposed essence or a predelineated ideal of Dasein" (HQT, 18). Such an analysis will unveil a number of structures which form a unity, if not a specific "whole," of Dasein, which Heidegger refers to as "care." 2) The unveiling of temporality as the "ontological meaning of care." 3) The reappropriation of the analyses of Division I in the clarification of the temporality of the existentialia. Dastur follows this path in a way that is both detailed and synthetic.

Dastur shows first that the question of temporality in *Being and Time* revolves around Dasein's Being-a-whole, its unitary character—a Being-a-whole which is not the classical "sum of the parts," nor an *archē* or a simple origin. On the contrary, Dasein's Being-a-whole reveals an organized plurality which lets its distinct items appear as distinct. These items are, of course, the existentialia. Analyzing the various developments of Division I, Dastur insists on two points: first, on the *dispersed* character of everyday Being-in-the-world, and second, on Dasein's oscillation between an "authentic" and an "inauthentic" mode of existence. Dastur places these terms in quotation marks in order to insist that Heidegger does not use them in a moral sense. Dastur insists on a crucial point, that authenticity and inauthenticity are modalities of Dasein's *existence*: the difference is therefore not a substantial one. In fact, "transposed to Dasein as a whole, this distinction accounts for the non-substantial character of Dasein," since it is because Dasein is a sheer potentiality-for-Being that it can be itself either authentically or inauthentically. Consequently, in authentic existence one does not reach another substantial domain; what is reached instead is everyday inauthentic existence itself, but having undergone a modification. Dastur notes that "to speak in terms of modification implies, to borrow again from Husserl's phenomenology, that there are not two substantially different 'subjects'—the They and the 'authentic' self—but rather two different ways of being the *same* subject" (HQT, 23). Therefore, "Dasein's authentic mode of Being, its 'authenticity,' in no way signifies a pure relation to oneself taking place outside of the world, but rather another way of Being in the world" (HQT, 27). For more clarifications on this crucial question, we refer the reader to Dastur's section on the translation of Heidegger's key terms (HQT, 73).

Dastur provides an illuminating reading of the second movement of *Being and Time*, where temporality is understood as the meaning of care. We know that Dasein is a being which is stretched or extended between the multiplicity of its existentialia, between the past of its facticity and the future of its projection. Dasein *is* the unity of a Being-thrown (*Geworfenheit*) and a projection

(*Entwurf*). Dastur interprets this "throw" (*Wurf*) as the very *dynamic* of a temporality. This is why, as she recalls quite pertinently, Heidegger calls the unity of care a temporalization, *Zeitigung*, giving it the dynamic, if not active, sense of a temporal movement. Time is a movement, an *élan*. "It could be said here that Heidegger has a dynamic, and no longer static, conception of the Being of man when he defines him as a Being-*thrown* in the world that always exists as a *projection* of itself" (HQT, xxv). Time is not a neutral context or frame in which events take place. It is rather the *mode of being* of an entity which exists in the mode of possibility. Dastur is then able to account for the primacy of the future in Heidegger's analysis of temporality. As Dastur explains, "the item of existentiality is made to bear all the weight of temporality: it is on the basis of existentiality that the authentic temporality of Dasein temporalizes itself; hence the privilege granted, no longer to the present, but instead to the *future*" (HQT, 35). This primordial movement (throw, projection) is a coming to oneself. Heidegger explains that the "letting-itself-*come-towards*-itself [*auf sich Zukommenlassen*]" represents "the primordial phenomenon of the future [*der Zu-kunft*]" (BT, 372/325). The authentic future (*Zukunft*) is a coming to oneself (*Zu-kunft*). Dastur then retraces the existential interpretation of the two other dimensions of temporality and their structural unity. Dasein's coming to itself implies the taking over or assumption (*Übernahme*) of its Being-thrown, since Dasein is always as *having-been*: Dasein is not "past", but *is* as having-been. This is why the resolute taking over and repetition of Being-thrown consists in "*Being* Dasein authentically *as it already was*" (BT, 372/326). Such is the existential sense of the past. With respect to the present, far from being the elusive point which the tradition since Aristotle speaks about, it is in fact disclosed by that very movement of projection and return, so that existential temporality should be understood in the following way: "Coming back to itself futurally, resoluteness brings itself into the situation by making present" (BT, 374/326). The temporal source of the existentialia analyzed in the first section—existentiality, facticity and fallenness—is thus clarified: Being-ahead-of-itself (future) already in a world (having-been) as alongside-intra-worldly-entities (present). Reciprocally, temporality appears in its eminently *ecstatic* character. For there is not a pre-given substantial subject, which, as Kant says, would include time within itself; rather, there is a threefold and ek-static movement of temporalization which constitutes the "self" and any "self-constancy." Dastur concludes that this ek-static character reveals the dynamic, rather than substantial, nature of temporality: "In calling the future, the having-been, and the present, 'ecstases of temporality,' it was an issue of emphasizing *temporalization* as a pure movement or event and not the stepping outside of oneself of a 'subject' which would first be 'in itself.'" (HQT, 37).

Dastur shows, in a third and final movement, that after the uncovering of care, and then of its temporal foundation in temporality, the issue consists in elaborating concretely the temporal meaning of the existentialia discussed in Division I of *Being and Time*. Following the circular movement of the existential analytic, one returns to the existentialia uncovered in the first division in order to reveal their temporal basis. Thus, the ek-stasis of the future will be said to constitute primarily—but not exclusively—the existential of the understanding, that of having-been the existential of "affectedness" (*Befindlichkeit*), and the ek-stasis of the present fallenness and discourse. Each of these ek-stases is, so to speak, "formal," that is, indifferent or neutral in relation to the "authentic" and "inauthentic" modes of Dasein. The structure is threefold, as Dastur demonstrates here: There is the "originary" (or neutral) temporality, and then there are the two modes of authentic and inauthentic temporality. The ek-stases can unfold in each of these modes. Thus, Being-ahead-of-itself, (*Sich-vorweg*), which designates the future in a neutral sense, can either be anticipation (*Vorlaufen*) (the "authentic" future) or awaiting (*Gewärtigen*) (the "inauthentic" future). The present can either be the moment of vision (*Augenblick*), or the making-present (*Gegenwärtigen*); having-been can either be repetition (*Wiederholung*), or *forgetting* (*Vergessenheit*). Dastur considers that such an existential interpretation of time ultimately reveals two dimensions missed by a tradition which has only understood time as an infinite sequence of nows: the finitude of time, and its givenness.

2. THE FINITE GIVENNESS OF TIME

Traditional interpretations miss the essential *finitude* of temporality by understanding time as an indefinite or infinite sequence of nows. But Heidegger will stress that "infinite time" proceeds and derives from finite time. "Only because primordial time is *finite* can 'derivative' time temporalize itself as *infinite*" (BT, 379/331). Indeed, time is *given*, or temporalizes itself, from the future. But, since the most extreme future is death, as that toward which and from which Dasein essentially exists, then death proves to be the secret source of temporality. Death is the heart of time. Such a primordial and finite source of temporality is covered up in the understanding of time as an infinite sequence of nows. However, Dastur shows that for Heidegger the finitude of time is in a sense disclosed, albeit negatively, in the everyday understanding of time. For the concealment of primordial temporality is not total or complete, since the inauthentic modalities of existence still manifest Dasein's essential constitution. The idea of an infinite passing of time, in which "one" never dies, already indicates, even if it attempts to negate it, the connection between time and death. Death is each time mine, and "my" time is defined by my relation to death as being my own alone. The very idea of "passing," which structures the ordinary understanding of time, betrays the futural coming of time. As Dastur puts it: "Only because Dasein is oriented toward the future can it understand the sequence of nows as an *irreversible succession*" (HQT, 50). In any event, finite temporality is what constitutes primordial time; according to Dastur, this is "Heidegger's essential thesis in *Being and Time*" (HQT, xxvi). Let us first underline what could be perceived as a paradox: the association of primordiality with finitude. The fact that temporality is given in the existential analytic a primordial function, that it is the horizon of the very understanding of Being, that is, of Dasein's essential constitution, the fact, then, that temporality is the primordial ontological meaning of care, does not mean that it would be "endless," unlimited, or infinite. Primordiality is not infinity. On the contrary, as Dastur insists, Heidegger thinks primordiality and finitude together. Finitude, far from being understood as in the Christian tradition, as some accident or fall, is here approached as being eminently positive, and is no longer referred to some infinite divine principle. Dastur is very clear on this point. Finitude is a *positive* feature. She writes that the "finitude of existence . . . should not be understood only in a negative sense. Indeed, finitude is not an accidental property of human reason, nor is it what differentiates man from a creating God, but is instead the necessity that man, in contrast with animals, projects the horizon of a possible understanding of what he depends on and 'has care of'—namely, the entity of which he is not the origin, that is, himself, others, and the world. Because man is not the origin of his own existence in the world, he is bound to understand and interpret what he finds *in front of* him, since it already existed *before* him. Finitude is consequently the very root of the understanding of being that characterizes man" (HQT, xxvi). Heidegger found this positive sense of finitude in Kant, more precisely, in the way in which Kant associates the finite faculties of rational beings with their a priori character. Unlike finite creatures, an infinite being would not *need* to anticipate the given in an a priori form. Heidegger makes such a point in *Kant and the Problem of Metaphysics*: because humans are not the origin of their own existence in the world, they must project the horizon of a possible understanding of that to which they are delivered over, namely, the entity which they are not the origin of, that is, themselves, others, and the world. As Dastur explains: "It is precisely because the human *intuitus* is *ontically* non-creative that it must be *ontologically* creative" (HQT, 60). Only a finite being is capable of projecting an understanding of Being, and thereby capable of "infinite" possibilities. Finitude is thus the source of the understanding of Being, and of all "infinity."

Indeed, to stress that temporality constitutes the ontological meaning of the entity that we are immediately indicates that human beings no longer "take part" in eternity. As early as 1924, in the lecture "The Concept of Time," Heidegger carefully and firmly distinguished all philosophical thinking of time from a theological problematic of eternity. To think time is not to think eternity. But to be defined in one's Being by time, to the exclusion of eternity, means to be approached as finite. Temporality then appears as the ontological meaning of an entity—Dasein—which is essentially toward-its-end, toward-death. We know what this means: not that Dasein will die one day, not that Dasein will reach its end one day, but rather that Dasein exists as dying, that is, exposed, each time, to its end. Dasein, then, is not immortal or infinite until it meets its "demise"; rather, it *"exists finitely"* (BT, 378/329). This finitude of time does not negate the fact that the future harbors an "unlimited" reservoir of possibilities. Time can be both finite and yet "infinite" in the possibilities it provides for Dasein. Dastur shows that what is essential "is not what time harbors, but rather the *way* in which it temporalizes itself" (HQT, 37). How, precisely, is time given? It is given in the mode of a "thrown projection," that is, as a "potentiality-for-Being whose future is closed and whose basis is 'null'" (HQT, 37). This twofold closure (*Entschluß*) represents the two limits or ends of Dasein: these, however, in accordance with the positive character of finitude, are to be thought as the horizon of Dasein's existence. The closure of the future is paradoxically what *opens* Dasein to itself most authentically. That "nullity" of its thrownness is that on the basis of which Dasein projects itself, indeed, it is that very thing that Dasein projects. The opening of Dasein is thus finite too, which indicates that, for Dasein, the opening of its existence must be thought in conjunction with a more hidden closure. "The Being of man, or Dasein, is only open to itself, to others, and to the world inasmuch as the possibility of the closure of all that is constantly threatens" (HQT, xxv–xxvi). More radically, even, the opening of Dasein's possibilities should be understood as made possible on the basis of a more primordial closure. Dastur concludes from this that we "therefore need to conceive of existence on the basis of mortality and of the opening on the basis of a *more primordial closure which is its source* and of which Dasein can never become the master" (HQT, xxvi, my emphasis). Humans are, first, mortals; human beings, Heidegger would later say, are to be called "the mortals."

That thought of a positive finitude will be further radicalized in Heidegger's work: from Dasein's finitude to the finitude of Being itself and the thought of *Ereignis*, this notion will, as it appears in the 1962 lecture, "Time and Being," definitively be severed from any reference to the infinite. Heidegger explains here that finitude "is no longer thought in terms of the relation to infinity." The issue is rather to think "finitude in itself: finitude, end, limit, one's own" (TB, 54). Finitude is here connected to the "limit," insofar as "limit" is understood in its Greek sense of *peras*, namely, not as "that at which something stops but . . . that from which something *begins its presencing* [*Wesen*]" (PLT, 154). Finitude in the early Heidegger, Dastur explains, "is still thought in relation to the transcendence of Dasein, whose being is a finite horizon, that is, in relation to the in-finitude of a self-projection which closes on itself, while the finitude of *Ereignis* comes from the intrinsic limit of destiny, which, as sending, must be secure in one's own abyssal withdrawal" (HQT, 65). This is why the issue becomes that of thinking time, no longer as a sequence of nows (homogeneous, objective time), and not even as the ek-static constitution of Dasein, but rather as the very presencing of presence, as the givenness of Being *and* time, a givenness which, as Dastur points out, is "a *sending*, that is, a gift without a 'subject' who gives" (HQT, 66). Certainly, as Dastur points out, whether in 1927 or in 1962, the question remains the same: it is the question of Being *and* time, the co-belonging of Being and time; but whereas this co-belonging was in 1927 sought after in the transcendence of Dasein, in a thinking of *Ereignis*, that is, in a thinking that attempts to think Being "without beings" (TB, 24), there can be no longer a reference to transcendence: to conceive of the presencing of Being as a transcendence of the totality of beings is still to represent Being on the basis of beings. When, in *Sein und Zeit*, Heidegger qualifies Being as "*the transcendens pure and simple* [*das transcendens schlechthin*]" (BT, 62/38), he understands Being as what lies beyond beings, that is, as still referred to beings for its determination. In this sense, this determination remains metaphysical and must be overcome. Instead, this co-belonging now pertains to a *givenness* that the traditional thinking of time has always covered over: the givenness one finds in the "*es gibt*" time, "*es gibt*" Being. Time "is" not; Being "is" not. But there is (*es gibt*) time, and there is (it gives) Being. "Being, when no longer thought of as the ground of beings, that is, when thought of in what is proper to it, is the gift of the unfolding of presence" (HQT, 66). It is in this meditation of givenness, of the "gift of time," approached in its essential duplicity or two-foldness, (between the giving and the given, the withdrawal which allows the giving) that, according to Dastur, Heidegger's thinking of Being and time culminate. That givenness of time is finite through and through: *Ereignis* is a sending (*Schicken*), that is, "a giving which gives only its very givenness and as such holds itself back and withdraws." This is why, Dastur explains, *Ereignis* "is in itself *Enteignis*, that is, the groundless ground of Being, its abyss. It is only at this point that Heidegger truly breaks with the idea of the absolute that governed the entire history of thought" (HQT, 65). Time is now to be thought not from the given, that is, the present (*Gegenwart*), but from givenness itself, that is, the coming into presence (*Anwesenheit*) which, as such, calls for humans to respond and correspond to it. This coming toward us characterizes more than just "the future," and more than the mere present: it is time as a whole which is this coming-toward-us, since the peculiar "absence" of the past, for instance, also comes toward us. As Heidegger explains, "even that which is no longer present presences [*west*] immediately in its absence . . . what has been presences [*Das Gewesen west*]" (TB, 13). Because this coming into presence, or presencing, is not an immediate presence, but instead takes place from a kind of distance and even absence, Dastur will stress that what is most proper to time is a givenness from a distance, conveyed in the German word *reichen*. That term conveys a sense of dimensionality, of a certain spaciousness of time that allows for its givenness to take place. This *Zeit-Raum* is "a self-extending, the [mutual] opening up of future, past and present . . . only thus can it make room, that is, provide space" (TB, 14). The opening of dimensionality provides the "reciprocal *play* of each of the dimensions of time—through which each gives the others and is given through them—" and represents the "unity" of time as the "fourth dimension" of time, which Heidegger calls *nearness*. As Dastur shows, it is this meditation on the finite dimensionality of the givenness of time to which Heidegger's reflection leads us.

We would like to extend our warmest thanks to Hugh Silverman and Graeme Nicholson, the co-editors of this series. We are also grateful to Professor Dastur for her kind encouragement and help in working out certain difficulties in the text. Bob Crease contributed at the early stages of this work. We thank the staff at SUNY Stony Brook, Virginia Massaro, Martha Smith, and Letitia Dunn, for their material and technical assistance, as well as Stephanie Schull for her assistance with our Preface.

Introduction
to the English Edition

◆

Dies, ja dies allein ist Rache *selber: des Willens Widerwilke gegen die* Zeit
und ihr "Es war".

This, indeed this alone, is what *revenge* is: The will's ill will against time
and its "it was."

—Nietzsche: *Thus Spoke Zarathustra*

Why another book on Heidegger, one might ask? Since the 1927 publication
of his major work, *Being and Time*, there have been numerous commentaries
on his works, not only in German but in most European languages and even a
non-European language, Japanese, that has acquired no less than five different
translations of *Being and Time*. Perhaps the reason for this book can be found
in Victor Farias's *Heidegger and Nazism*, published in the fall of 1987, which
sought to forbid any future readings of a work which he considered to be, as
a whole, the expression of National Socialist ideology. In order to answer these
accusations, it seemed urgent to me to undertake a reading of Heidegger's
texts that would be as devoid of prejudices as possible *before* being able to
answer the (certainly crucial) question of the relation between his thought and
his political engagement of 1933 in the National Socialist party.

I had personally undertaken such a reading well before the publication of
Farias's book, at the time, in the middle of the sixties, when I decided to study
in Germany, at Freiburg, a university where Heidegger did his studies and
taught, first alongside his master, Edmund Husserl, then as his replacement.
For indeed—is it necessary to recall it?—Heidegger's political past was not
ignored at that time, and the question had already arisen of how a thinker of
this magnitude could have espoused such a political movement. Was there in

Heidegger's philosophy anything—a stand, a claim—that could have prepared or explained his encounter with the racist ideology of the N.S.D.A.P, a party which, we must remember, was called the National Socialist Party of the German Workers? This question has been posed by intellectuals, and French intellectuals in particular, ever since Heidegger's de-nazification trial, which was organized under the control of the French forces of occupation in July 1945. That trial's report, submitted in September 1945, concluded—we must note—that Heidegger's philosophy was radically incompatible with the Nazi doctrine.[1]

But in order to pose this question properly, it is necessary to *read* well, that is, to be receptive to a thought without classifying it too quickly among opinions which are already known and recorded, and without reducing it, through one of those unsubstantiated accusations that are customary to prosecutors and moralists, to the then prevailing ideology. In a public seminar held in November 1951, at the invitation of students and professors of the University of Zürich, Heidegger himself declared: "I believe that we must first learn how to read again, to read the words of the thinkers and poets. This very simple thing— to learn how to read, read the words of the thinkers and poets—this basic preparatory schooling is what would allow me, in the most general sense, to say what I would like to say"; for, he added: "One cannot think without thinking historically, in a profound sense, that is, learning how to read, bringing once again the word and speech into proximity to human beings."[2] One can see, then, that attempting to read Heidegger cannot mean abstracting his "discourse" from history by giving it an "atemporal" sense, but, on the contrary, hearing what it tells us about our era, in the guise not of *ideological positions* but rather of a *meditative questioning*.

To read Heidegger means, therefore, coming to terms with his meditative questioning, to hearken to what he himself tells us is his fundamental question. Surprisingly, this question has not been *thematically* investigated. Indeed, to my knowledge only one thesis[3] bears on the problem of the relation between Being and time, even though, as everyone knows, this problem is the "center" of Heidegger's "philosophy."

Now, Heidegger's meditative questioning, which cannot be reduced to a definite ideological position, is concerned with the whole philosophical tradition of thought, insofar as it has been determined by Aristotle—who in this respect followed the lessons of his master, Plato, the first philosopher in the strict sense of the term—as *philosophy*, that is, as a thought of Being, as *ontology*. In this sense, the Western tradition begins, as Plato noted (cited by Heidegger in the very first pages of *Being and Time*), when "one stops telling stories" (*Sophist*, 242 c.), that is, when one stops explaining one entity by way of another entity, according to the mythological or theological mode of thought which has recourse to one or more supreme beings as the origin of beings that are present-at-hand. Ontology, that is, the Platonic-Aristotelian science of Being, remains with what is present-at-hand, with the *entity*—*to on* in Greek—as such (*on hē on*), and determines it in terms of its essence. Philosophy is therefore that specific form of thought which claims to account for the entity as such, without having recourse to any other origin than that which is strictly *given*. Remaining with what is present-at-hand constitutes the originality of philosophy as compared to mythical, theogonical, or theological modes of thought. This statement characterizes the way in which philosophy understands itself, that is, as this Western mode of thought that heralds the triumph of logos over mythos, of the rational over the irrational.

Heidegger, on the contrary, begins with this traditional understanding that philosophy has of itself in order to put it into question. He is thus also led, as were Plato and Aristotle, to pose the question "What is Being?" but in a new sense; not in order to inquire into what constitutes the essence of any entity as such, that is, what is present-at-hand [*donné présent*] but in order to inquire into the very condition of possibility of given *presence* [*présence donnée*], which is also the condition of the possibility of the "science" of presence, that is, philosophy, namely, ontology as defined by Plato and Aristotle. It is therefore not a matter, for Heidegger, of inscribing his fundamental question in the field of "philosophy"—which has already been circumscribed—but on the contrary of questioning the condition of its possibility, that is, the very condition of the possibility of *Western rationality*. This is what he will later call "The Return to the Ground of Metaphysics," the title of the Preface added in 1949 to the 1929 lecture "What Is Metaphysics?" This fundamental question concerning the condition of the possibility of the understanding of Being by the Greek philosophers and their descendants, the modern philosophers of the West, as *constant presence*, is a question bearing on the relation—never made explicit in this Western tradition—between time and Being. What makes possible the understanding of Being from a specific dimension of time, that is, the present? This is the question, in its most basic form, which is at the origin of *Being and Time*. This title itself should not be misunderstood; in his 1929 *Kant and the Problem of Metaphysics* Heidegger emphasizes that it is the small word "and" which conceals within itself the central problem (KPM, 165). Indeed, the issue for Heidegger is not to oppose time and becoming to Being, as was still the case for Nietzsche, who writes, for instance, in *The Twilight of the Idols*, "Heraclitus will remain eternally right with his assertion that being is an empty fiction,"[4] but on the contrary to bring to light the hidden connection between what we call "Being" and time. Heidegger goes as far as to speak of an "intrinsic co-belonging of Being and time," which is a decisive way of challenging the traditional equivalence between being and eternity, Being and atemporality.

But if ontology, the science of Being, must thus be referred back to the condition of its possibility, namely, to a certain understanding of Being on the basis of or within the horizon of time, what is implied is that the very basis of this ontology must be questioned in the context of what Heidegger will call "fundamental ontology." What makes rational discourse, or Western logic, possible? Heidegger answers this question by showing that the philosophical question of Being is rooted in a particular entity which is capable of questioning, not only about other entities, but also about the entity that it is itself. The understanding of Being is a human mode of Being, or *comportment*: the root of Being is therefore man, that is, that entity who has the idea of Being. One can see here to what extent the "ontological" question becomes, for Heidegger, the most "concrete" one: it is not a question about the most abstract generalities, but a question that concerns the very entity who raises it, and includes the questioner itself.

In "What is Metaphysics?" Heidegger insists on the fact that, contrary to a scientific question, which always bears on something objective, a metaphysical question has the peculiarity of concerning the entity that raises it, and puts its own existence into question by inquiring into Being and non-Being, time, death, and so on. However, Heidegger does not call that entity, which is implicated in the philosophical questions it raises, "subject" nor even simply "man," but rather "Dasein," a term used in German to translate the Latin *existentia*, and meaning literally Being-there. Heidegger will give this term an even more specific sense, since it no longer designates existence in general, but strictly the mode of Being of the human being. The latter should thus not be understood as an existent among others, in the sense of simply being there, in the midst of other beings, such as animals, plants, or stones, but on the contrary as a particular entity "which is in some sense all things," as Aristotle said of the human soul. This is an entity for which "Being is at issue," open to Being and to the world, capable of "understanding" it, and which is not isolated or closed upon itself. Heidegger considers this *opening* to itself and to other entities to be constitutive of what is proper to *Existenz* (existence), giving this term— which *exclusively* designates the human entity—the strong sense of a non-substantial entity, continually "in projection," which cannot be conceived, as modern philosophy has done since Descartes, as a "subject," that is, as an autonomous substance that, according to its traditional definition, "does not need anything other than itself to subsist." On the contrary, for Heidegger, ecstatic existence, which characterizes human existence, has the need to go outside of itself (this is the proper sense of the term *existere*) and only exists in the threefold relation it has with itself, with other existences, and with the world. It is therefore not an entity centered around itself, as the modern subject is, but rather, as Heidegger will explicitly state in a footnote of a text dedicated to Husserl in 1929 (ER, 99), an essentially "excentric" being, since it is nothing outside of the *relation* to the other than itself.

Indeed, in order to account for the rationality of the Western scientific project, insofar as it is rooted in philosophy as a science of Being, it is not sufficient, according to Heidegger, to have recourse to a conception of man, that is, an anthropology that sees man as a living being endowed with reason—this traditional definition of man as *zōon logon ekhon*, or *animal rationale*, is the basis of its modern definition as "subject." This is what is interesting in Heidegger's thought: it does not content itself with simply presupposing the existence of reason, by conceiving it as a "natural" disposition innate to man, for this is a tautological manner of explaining rationality by reason, which ultimately explains nothing. For Heidegger, the traditional definition of man as a being composed of animality and rationality is a definition which is not original; it is a metaphysical definition precisely because it conceives the essence of man as the unexplainable union of two opposites, the body and the soul, the sensible and the intelligible, nature and spirit. It was, in fact, through this refusal to understand man as a living being among others in the context of what one might call a general "biology"—in the literal sense of a "science of life"—that Heidegger, from the outset (from his courses in the early twenties), distanced himself from the prevailing "philosophy of life" as well as from the *rassische Weltanschauung*, the racist conception of the world which lay at the basis of National Socialist ideology. Biologism cannot account for what constitutes the humanity of man, and Heidegger went so far as to say in 1946, in his *Letter on Humanism*, that Western philosophy, that is, metaphysics, radically ignored the *humanitas* as such by constantly thinking it on the basis of *animalitas*.[5]

However, how are we to conceive of man if it is no longer possible to conceive of him in the modern sense, or in the traditional or ancient sense as *animal rationale*? Heidegger's answer is succinct: man has to be thought as *care*, and the ontological meaning of care is *temporality*. If man is neither a substance, a "thing," nor an animal (even endowed with a specific difference, reason), it is because he is a being-in-projection, a temporality, a movement or *élan*. It could be said here that Heidegger has a dynamic, and no longer static, conception of the being of man when he defines him as a being-*thrown* in the world that always exists as a *projection* of itself. Heidegger calls "care" the structure which articulates the "past" of the being which is always already thrown into the world with the "future" of self-projecting and the "present" of being alongside such or such an entity—not in the "moral" sense of the term, but as a designation of the fundamentally "excentric" being of man. Man exists only in care and concern for itself, and for the other than itself, the German *Sorge*, like the Latin *cura*, having the meanings of "care" and "concern."

However, to say that the Being of man is temporality and that his substance lies in his existence is immediately to conceive the Being of man as a *Being essentially toward death*, and no longer participating, in part—his rational part—in "eternity." This thinking of mortality is not, for Heidegger, pessimistic or nihilistic, but rather the recognition of what is distinctively positive in existence. The Being of man, or Dasein, is only open to itself, to others, and to the world, inasmuch as the possibility of the closure of all that is constantly threatens. We therefore need to conceive of existence on the basis of mortality, and of the opening on the basis of a more primordial closure which is its source and of which Dasein can never become the master.

As thrown into the world and Being-toward-death, human existence is thus essentially finite: ecstatical temporality is a *finite temporality*, and it is this finite temporality that constitutes primordial time; this is Heidegger's essential thesis in *Being and Time*, which opposes the ordinary understanding of time as a sequence of nows. This finitude of existence, however, should not be understood only in a negative sense. Indeed, finitude is not an accidental property of human reason, nor is it what differentiates man from a creating God, but is instead the necessity that man, in contrast with animals, projects the horizon of a possible understanding of what he depends on and "has care of"—namely, the entity of which he is not the origin, that is, himself, others, and the world. Because man is not the origin of his own existence in the world, he is bound to understand and interpret what he finds *in front of* him, since it already existed *before* him. Finitude is consequently the very root of the understanding of Being that characterizes man, and the *finite temporality of existence is therefore the basis of the idea of Being on which Western rationality is founded.* This essential finitude is the basis for what Heidegger calls the "historicality" of Dasein, that is, not the fact that it can be the object of historical science, but the fact that it exists in an intrinsically historical way, that is, by having its inherited possibilities transmitted to it when coming into the world and which it has to take on anew.

At the basis of ontology, of this science of Being which defines the philosophical project, that is, the project of Western rationality as a whole, there is therefore a comportment of man insofar as his Being is defined essentially as a temporal-ecstatic existence. If time is indeed the horizon of the comprehensibility of Being, then the science of Being is a "temporal"[6] science, that is, a science that cannot be founded on an atemporal reason or on an eternal truth. Does this mean that Heidegger joined the camp of relativism? To claim the historicality of truth allows Heidegger to reveal the hidden existential origin of ontological concepts which are thought to have a universal scope and an atemporal meaning. It thus makes clear that philosophy is not a "pure" theory and that ontology can never be completely divorced from its concrete existential roots. This does not imply the equivalence of all points of view but rather—since there is no philosophy devoid of a point of view and rationality is never neutral—that philosophy, as such, is "engaged."

This is a frightening conclusion, for it does not protect philosophy from error and no longer permits—that was the philosophical "dream" itself, from Plato to Husserl—a radical distinction between the *thought of essence* and the *opinion on facts*, the ontological and the ontical. Heidegger thus shows, by an unexpected move that seems paradoxically Marxian,[7] that philosophizing can no longer consist in taking refuge in pure theory but rather implies the risk of a practical existential engagement.

It would then be on the basis of such an essence of philosophy, as Heidegger saw it in 1927, that one would have to understand his 1933 political engagement, an engagement which can no longer be seen as a mere accident nor a pure opportunism. As is now clear, "to judge" Heidegger and his political engagement on the basis of the presuppositions of his own thought (a thought which is never "neutral" with respect to history) is in no way an attempt to excuse him.

Françoise Dastur

Presentation

———◆———

Any kind of polemics fails from the outset to assume the attitude of thinking.

—WCT, 113

For those who wish to form an opinion on Heidegger's thought, this short book has for its sole ambition to provide reference points meant to guide the serious reading of his texts. The guiding thread, which as it were leaps into view, is the problematic that Heidegger always took to be his fundamental question: the relation between Being and time.

The whole originality of Heidegger's thought turns on the clarification of the *Temporal* meaning of what the Western tradition from its inception (Parmenides, Plato, and Aristotle) has called "Being." Heidegger begins with a simple observation: *ousia* (Being, or rather "Beingness"[1]) is understood by the Greeks as constant presence. Far from it being the case that time is a property of what is, a criterion on the basis of which regions of Being can be differentiated (the temporal as opposed to the intemporal or eternal), it is on the contrary the idea of Being itself which is thought within the horizon of time and placed in relation to a determined mode of time, the *present*. Starting in 1927, in his magnum opus, *Being and Time*, Heidegger advances the thesis of a *Temporality of Being*, which radically invalidates the metaphysical identification of Being with eternity.

Heidegger, not satisfied merely with putting forward a general ontological thesis, is interested in pursuing a "concrete" ontological investigation; it is necessary to clarify the Temporal meaning of Being by taking a determinate being [*être*] or, rather, an "entity" [*étant*] as a starting point. Heidegger chooses as his starting point the entity which understands Being, that is, the entity for which alone "there is" Being—namely, man himself. But Heidegger refuses to name man "consciousness" or "subject," following modern denominations, and instead chooses the untranslatable *Dasein*. In contrast with the modern subject, which is closed in upon itself, man as Dasein is essentially defined as *existence*; that is, as Being outside itself, as having an *ecstatic* structure. Heidegger calls this essential *opening* of the Being of man *care*, as a result of an *existential analytic* which is, however, only provisional.

Heidegger's concern is indeed to bring to light the truly temporal meaning of existence as a uniquely human mode of Being. Now, Dasein as existing is finite, that is, mortal; it is *Being toward death*, which implies that finitude is not an accident of its "immortal" essence but the very basis of its existence. This is why the temporality of Dasein is not to be understood as the Being *in* time of an essentially atemporal subject but as the deployment in three directions of a single opening. If Heidegger does maintain the classical analysis of time into a threefold structure, still, past, present, and future no longer designate a succession of nows on the "line" of time but instead equiprimordial modalities of existence, or *ecstases*. One of these ecstases, however, is privileged: the future. Indeed, the "authentic"[2] meaning of the temporality of a finite being springs from the future, that is, from the anticipation of death. Thus Heidegger arrives at the thesis of the *finitude* of primordial time in opposition to the classical thesis of the infinitude of physical time.

On this basis it becomes possible to repeat the provisional existential analysis by exhibiting the temporal meaning of Dasein's structures, or *existentialia*, that characterize it in its *everydayness*. But, in order to account for the enigma of everydayness, that is, for the temporal *stretching along* of Dasein *between* birth and death, one must first understand that the question of the connectedness of existence has meaning only for one who lives dispersed and not for one who takes over inherited factical possibilities; that is, for the one who is in the true sense *historical*, existing as finite temporality. Yet, concerned Dasein "reckons" with time and understands itself as existing *in* time. One must thus explain the *genesis* of the idea of successive and infinite time on the basis of the primordial temporality of Dasein. Now, *ordinary* time is not related to primordial time, as the objective time of nature is to the subjective time of the soul; the virtue of the Heideggerian problematic, instead, is that it negates the very subject-object distinction. There is Being, and there is time, only insofar as there is Dasein, which in no way means that Being and time are "products" of our understanding, but rather that only with, and as it were in Dasein—in the clearing of the *Da*—can there be the happening of any world at all, and any history at all. The *ordinary* concept of time (ordinary is not opposed here to philosophical, but characterizes the *public, open* aspect of time) originates in a levelling off of primordial time, by which the latter is less identified with space, as Bergson claimed, than referred to the world of everyday concern and reduced to the pure subsistence of an infinite sequence of *nows*. Hence the idea of an infinite, successive, and irreversible time. But this ordinary representation of time has its *own legitimacy*, that of public time, which does correspond to a mode of being of Dasein: everyday concern. Yet, what time truly is cannot be understood on the basis of public time, for in public time the meaning of temporalization undergoes a fundamental modification; it is on the basis of the present, that is, a punctual now (and no longer on the basis of the future), that the other temporal dimensions are deployed.

However, the analysis of the temporality of Dasein and the demonstration of the derivative character of our usual representation of time do not yet answer the fundamental question of the Temporality of being. To that end, one would have to show how the understanding of being is made possible by the ecstatic temporality of Dasein; in other words, how the idea of Being in its manifold senses is constituted on the basis of time as "place." Heidegger left *Being and Time* unfinished, and this program was left unfulfilled. Yet, he continued to pursue it in his courses of the same period. The 1962 lecture "Time and Being," which takes up again the program of the unpublished third section of Division I of *Being and Time*, offers a quite different perspective on the Temporality of being than the one sketched out in 1927. Now, the *co-appropriation* of time and Being is thought, beyond all metaphysical distinctions, through the equally untranslatable term *Ereignis*.

1
◆

The Temporality of Being as Basic Question

> We do not question Being alone, and we do not question time alone either. Neither do we question Being and also time; rather we question their *inner co-belonging* and what springs from it.
>
> —GA 31, 118

The young Heidegger, leaving behind the study of theology for that of philosophy, at first dedicated his efforts to logical problems. Indeed, the tide of ideas unleashed by the publication in 1901 of Husserl's *Logical Investigations* determined the form as well as the content of Heidegger's first writings, from his 1914 dissertation, *The Doctrine of Judgment in Psychologism*, to his habilitation thesis of 1916, *The Theory of Categories and Signification in Duns Scotus*, which is governed by the Husserlian idea of a pure, a priori grammar. Already at that time, however, Heidegger was becoming aware of the importance of the historical dimension. In the preface of his dissertation, he thanked one of his professors (the historian Finke) for having awakened "in the mathematician resistant to history love and understanding for it," and he chose to devote his trial lecture of 27 July 1915 to "The Concept of Time in Historical Science."

This lecture is Heidegger's first text devoted to time. But we are still very far from the problematic of *Being and Time*. The work pursues an epistemological inquiry aimed at establishing the specificity of the concept of time in historical science, in opposition to the concept of time in the physical sciences, which Heidegger investigates in the first part of this lecture. Recalling his semester of studies in mathematics and physics, he attempts to show that, from Galileo to Einstein, the conception of time in physics has not changed; the function of time being to make measurement possible, it constitutes a necessary moment in the definition of movement which is the very object of physical science. But in order to make measurement possible, time itself must become

1

measurable, which can only happen if it is conceived as a uniform flow; that is to say, as identified with space. Opposed to this homogenized and spatialized time, which has become a mere parameter, is historical time, which is characterized, on the contrary, by its qualitative heterogeneity. Historical science does not work with quantities, even when occupied with establishing chronology, but works instead only with significations and values—which explains why it cannot be reduced to the epistemological model of the natural sciences. Heidegger, developing a theory of physical time which is not without similarities to Bergson's theory in *Essai sur les données immédiates de la conscience* (cited by Heidegger in both of his theses), shares Dilthey's view of the difference between the respective methods of the natural and the human sciences. But, over and above the purely epistemological problem, some ontological considerations already appear about what constitutes "true" time, which is not physical time, and which is characterized by diversity and heterogeneity. However, time is still grasped in its opposition to eternity, as is testified to by the quotation by Meister Eckhart which Heidegger made the slogan of his lecture: "Time is what *changes* and *evolves*, eternity remains simple."

a) Time and Eternity

Now, it is precisely this—seemingly unavoidable—opposition between time and eternity that Heidegger begins by rejecting in a lecture of July 1924, "The Concept of Time," given before the Marburg Society of Theology. It is no longer a question of considering that "time finds its meaning in eternity" but, on the contrary, of "understanding time on the basis of time itself," according to an approach to the problem which is no longer theological but properly philosophical. Speaking before theologians, Heidegger is concerned with distinguishing the dimension of *thought* from the dimension of *faith*. That same concern had motivated him to claim, in a course of the winter semester, 1921–22, that "philosophy *itself* is as such atheistic when it understands itself radically" (GA 61, 198), which means that the philosopher does not behave in a religious way when he thinks even though he may be a religious person.

In a lecture given in March 1927 in Tübingen, Heidegger characterizes very clearly the relation between philosophy and theology as one between two sciences which are absolutely different from one another. Philosophy is the science of Being, which Being is not something given beforehand for subsequent scientific investigation, but rather the dimension on the basis of which any given as such appears. Theology is not an ontological but an *ontical* science, which is to say, it is the science of an entity antecedently given for investigation, and is in this respect much closer to positive sciences such as mathematics or chemistry than to philosophy. Faith is what constitutes the positivity of theology, a mode of existence radically different from the one which gives rise to philosophy. Faith is a mode of existence that is not freely chosen but results from revelation, while the attitude at the basis of philosophy is one of taking responsibility for one's Being as a whole. Heidegger then goes so far as to speak of faith as the "mortal enemy" of philosophy. If one can speak of a commonality of philosophy and theology, it is solely because theology, like any other positive science, needs philosophy to determine the ontological domain of its own concepts. As for philosophy, it in no way needs theology, which explains why it attempts neither to fight nor to annex it: the very idea of a "Christian philosophy," Heidegger concludes, is a square circle. Only the dimension of faith and of what is revealed through it allows for access to a genuine eternity which is equivalent to God. For the philosopher, eternity is nothing other than the empty concept of a permanent being, which, far from being the origin of time, is in fact *derived* from our ordinary experience of temporality.

It is thus out of the question to seek the origin of time elsewhere than in ourselves, in the temporality that we are, which is why Heidegger stresses at the end of his lecture that one should not try to define time as being this or that, but rather to transform the question "*What* is time?" into the question "*Who* is time?"—that is, to wonder whether we *ourselves* are not time. This is the only way to "speak temporally of time," instead of hypostatizing it as a being different from us which would attribute an *identity* to us that would precisely negate our temporal character. This thesis—repeated several times in the lecture as "Dasein is time"—anticipates the problematic of the existential analytic which Heidegger developed in 1927 in *Being and Time*, and which this 1924 lecture presents in a strikingly succinct way. Rather than summarize this extremely dense text, I shall limit myself to exhibiting the necessity of what Heidegger himself calls the "detour" which, from the question of time, leads us to the question of the entity that we ourselves are and which Heidegger is already calling Dasein—meaning by this, he explains, "the Being of this entity that we know as human life." For, it is not enough to note, with Aristotle and after him St. Augustine, that the *measure* of time is only possible through the intermediary of the soul or the mind. One needs furthermore to recognize that human beings have a very peculiar relation to time, since only on their basis can the nature of time be deciphered. Human beings are not *in* time as are things of nature, but are fundamentally temporal; they *are* time.

This is what we learn from the phenomenological analysis of our experience of the measure of time. Indeed, the clock does not indicate duration, which is the amount of elapsing time, but only the "now" as it is assigned each time in relation to present, past, or future action. Therefore, I can only read time off the clock by referring to the "now" that I am, which comes from a temporality which is "mine" and which pre-exists all instruments intended to measure it. The Dasein which is each time "mine"—in the sense that it is constitutively an "I am"—is therefore not simply *in* time, understood as that in which the events of the world take place; rather, time itself is the proper *modality* of Dasein's Being. But this authentic temporality of Dasein, which Heidegger distinguishes from what in *Being and Time* he will call the *intratemporality* of intra-worldly things, is only accessible to Dasein when Dasein understands itself as a *mortal* being; that is, when it anticipates its own end as that which constitutes the extreme possibility of its Being and not as a mere accident which would befall it from the outside. Through this anticipation of death that Heidegger recognizes as the authentic future—not what is *not yet* present, but the dimension on the basis of which there can be a present and a past—Dasein *gives its time to itself.* It then becomes clear that the original relation to time cannot be that of measurement. For, in what Heidegger calls the anticipation of death, *Vorlaufen*, or literally running ahead into death, the point is not to wonder how much time remains before one's death, but for Dasein to seize its own death as a possibility at each moment.

Heidegger discovered the conception of original temporality as authentic future in the first epistle of St. Paul to the Thessalonians, which he commented upon in a course given during the winter semester, 1920–21, *Introduction to the Phenomenology of Religion.* The Christian experience involves a new conception of eschatology in the sense that the authentic Christian relation to parousia, that is, to the second coming to presence of Christ, signaling the end of time, is not the *awaiting* of a future event but the *readiness for* the imminence of this coming. Having a relation to parousia means being ready in the present rather than being in expectation of an event that has not yet taken place: the question "When?" has become the question "*How* to live?"—namely, in the mode of readiness. In fact, what really interests Heidegger in the original Christian experience is not the fact that it is a faith in this or that content of revelation, but that it is an experience of life in its *facticity*, that is, a life which takes no theoretical distance from itself but understands itself within the realm of its own unfolding. Because this life does not attempt to provide an "objective" representation of existence by means of chronological reference points and calculable contents, it remains delivered over to an indeterminate future and to the unmasterable character of time; it situates time, considered as a whole, less in the *chronos* than in the *kairos*, in the opportune moment, the moment of decision. The kairological characters characterize life in its facticity precisely because they determine its relation to time, which is one of enactment effectuation (GA 61, 137). In 1924, Heidegger calls this nonobjectifiable relation of effectuation with time *historicality*, appropriating a term that Dilthey himself borrowed from Yorck von Wartenberg (see *Being and Time*, paragraph 77). At that time, Heidegger was extremely interested in Dilthey, whose correspondence with Yorck von Wartenberg between 1877 and 1897 had just been published (in 1923): it has recently been discovered (in 1986) that in April 1925, in Kassel, Heidegger devoted a series of ten lectures to Dilthey in which he stressed, in contrast to the ahistorical character of the Husserlian phenomenology, the importance but also the limits of Dilthey's "historical" problematic. From Dilthey, Heidegger retains the idea that life understands itself on the basis of itself, that "it has a hermeneutic structure"; he calls the last course he gave in Freiburg during the summer semester 1923 *Hermeneutics of Facticity*, understanding by this expression the self-articulation of facticity insofar as it has the ability of understanding and interpreting itself. Yet, it is also in this course in Freiburg that Heidegger abandons Dilthey's vocabulary of the "philosophy of life" in favor of that of existential analysis; the term Dasein first appears, whereas the winter semester, 1921–22, course spoke only of life in its facticity. The limits of Dilthey's thought are the same as those of a philosophy of life that, because it opposes nature and history, being and life, does not sufficiently question the *entity* which is intrinsically historical and which Heidegger no longer conceives, as the tradition did, as a *living being* endowed with reason, as *animal rationale*, but rather as a particular *being* which is granted the privilege of understanding the being that it is as well as the beings that it is not—that is, as Dasein.

To give up the attempt to master time by means of calculation (that is, to objectify it in the form of a time which is only for everyone because it is for no one, which Heidegger names the time of the "*they*") is paradoxically the only way to "have" time as authentically mine. Time thus turns out to be the true principle of individuation, that is, that on the basis of which Dasein is in each case mine. But if each Dasein, in the relation with death, finds itself alone in the face of that which constitutes the unique character of one's destiny, still, this extreme isolation, in which each Dasein experiences what cannot be shared, is also what renders each Dasein identical to all others. The finitude of authentic time is then no longer contrasted with an eternity that would include it; the uniqueness of the temporality of all existence no longer stands out against the background of an infinite in which it would come to abolish itself. On the contrary, as Heidegger stressed in *Being and Time* (BT, 479/427, note xiii), the traditional concept of eternity understands eternity as a "permanent now," or *nunc stans*, which itself derives from the *ordinary* understanding of time as an infinite sequence of punctual nows. If, on the basis of Heidegger's approach to time, something like eternity is still thinkable, it would have an entirely different meaning and be based upon a temporality thought in a more original way. Time can no longer be thought of on the basis of eternity, but, on the contrary, eternity must be thought of on the basis of time.

b) THE QUESTION OF BEING AND THE QUESTION OF TIME

The questions of facticity and temporality, however, were not the first to concern Heidegger; as we have seen, his earliest concern was with the clarification of logical problems. When, at the end of his life, Heidegger attempted retrospectively to reconstruct his own "path of thinking"—as he had already done in his dialogue with the Japanese professor in 1954 (OWL, 6–7), the letter he wrote in response to Father Richardson's questions in 1962 (HPT, x), the short autobiographical text dedicated in 1963 to his publisher Hermann Niemeyer for the celebration of the latter's eightieth birthday (TB, 75), or his 1969 presentation at the congress commemorating the thirtieth anniversary of Husserl's death—he continued to identify, as the point of departure of his thought, Aristotle's *to on legetai pollakhos* ("Being is said in many ways"), which Husserl's teacher Franz Brentano used as an epigraph to his 1862 dissertation, *On the Manifold Meaning of Being According to Aristotle*. This book, which Heidegger received in 1907 from the hands of Conrad Gröber, his protector and friend, was his first philosophical reading, one which would determine the orientation of his thought toward the question of the *meaning* of Being. Aristotle distinguishes four apparently incompatible meanings of Being: Being by its own nature or as accident, as that which is potentiality or actually, as the true, and as conforming to the schemata of the categories. Heidegger's question bears on the basic and guiding signification which rules over this multiplicity of meanings, which Aristotle simply enumerated. But while Brentano privileged the categorial signification of Being over the others, Heidegger, who looked for a solution to the questions raised by his reading of Brentano's dissertation in Husserl's *Logical Investigations*, came to attribute a decisive importance to Being as the true.

In 1973, in his last seminar in Zähringen devoted to Husserl, Heidegger most clearly described the decisive contribution made by the *Logical Investigations* on the question of the meaning of Being. "With his analysis of categorial intuition, Husserl has freed Being from its assignment to judgment" (QIV, 315). Indeed, to say with Husserl in his Sixth Investigation (§ 44) that "Being is neither a judgment nor a real component of judgment" is to go against the entire philosophical tradition by refusing to identify Being with the copula of judgment which merely signifies it. Rather, Being is *given as such* in the fulfilling intuition which comes to authenticate the intention of signification. According to Husserl, Being is not a mere concept, a pure abstraction, but is given to a categorial sight analogous to sensible sight. In a course of 1925, *History of the Concept of Time: Prolegomena*, Heidegger included in the great discoveries of Husserlian phenomenology (besides that of intentionality and of the originary meaning of the a priori) that of the *categorial intuition*. Its signification is crucial to the *ontological* relevance of phenomenology, since it tends, against all nominalism, to extend the idea of objectivity to the sphere of generality and to show that the legitimation of ideal objects pertains to a phenomenological analysis of the intentional acts of signification and fulfillment. Heidegger thus saw in the Husserlian theory of self-evidence—understood as the *act* of identification of what is intended [*vise*] and intuited (and not, following the tradition, as the sign of certain experiences, specifically those of judgment)—and in the ensuing theory of truth as identity between what is intended and what is intuited (*Logical Investigations* 6, §39), a proximity with the Aristotelian concept of truth as found in Chapter 10 of Book Theta of the *Metaphysics*, where it is said that truth can occur in the assertive grasp of a thing and not simply in the predicative judgment, which Heidegger saw as the high point of ancient thought. "Phenomenology thus breaks with the restriction of the concept of truth to relational acts, to judgments. . . . Without being explicitly conscious of it, phenomenology returns to the broad concept of truth whereby the Greeks (Aristotle) could call true even perception as such and the simple perception of something" (HCT, 55/73).

If, according to Heidegger, Husserl joins Aristotle on this point, it is because he challenged the traditional definition of truth, according to which the proposition is the locus of truth, when the issue, on the contrary, is to understand, as Heidegger firmly states in his winter semester, 1925–26, course, *Logik: Die Frage nach der Wahrheit*, "The proposition is not the locus of truth; rather, truth is the locus of the proposition" (GA 21, 135). Truth thus appears as a dimension of Being itself rather than of judgment; furthermore, to characterize Being as "the true" is to give it its genuine determination, in the sense that, for Aristotle, something truly *is* that can be disclosed in a purely assertive grasp, *adding* nothing to what is but simply *presenting* it. But Aristotle himself does not question the meaning of this identity between Being and truth; that is, he does not bring out the properly *temporal* character of the *presentation* of what is in a purely assertive grasp. Consequently the essentially temporal determination of the meaning of Being as *presence* is ignored (GA 21, paragraph 14). The one and only philosopher in the entire history of ontology to have sensed something of this intrinsic connection between the understanding of Being and time is Kant (GA 21, 194; also BT, 45/23), which explains why Heidegger engaged in a thorough dialogue with Kant before and after 1927, in courses (the second part of *Logik* in 1925–26 is devoted to Kant, after Husserl and Aristotle, and in 1927–28, the entirety of the course of the winter semester treats of *The Phenomenological Interpretation of Kant's Critique of Pure Reason*) that resulted in a book, *Kant and the Problem of Metaphysics*, in 1929.

In his theory of the schematism of the pure concepts of the understanding, Kant shows that the understanding "can in no way operate except in being essentially referred to time" (GA 25, 430), since the mediating representations or schemes which allow the application of categories to appearances are a priori determinations of time. Kant has thus sensed, without truly being able to see it, the function assigned to time in any act of understanding; and if he was only able to sense it, it was essentially because of his conception of time itself, which he inherited from the philosophical tradition and in particular from Leibniz and Newton. Indeed, since Aristotle, time has been defined as physical time, the time of the objective world. As long as one holds to such a conception of time, that is to say, as long as time is not understood as being truly Dasein itself, it remains impossible to see the intrinsic connection of any act of consciousness with time. Heidegger proposes, on the basis of a conception of time that is radically different from the one which rules the tradition from beginning to end, to thematize the *Temporal* structure of logical phenomena within the framework of that which, under the name of "phenomenological chronology," could constitute a new fundamental discipline of philosophy. The new discipline would have nothing in common with the scientific discipline of the same name, which belongs to the historical sciences. The issue would be to show how phenomena that do not necessarily take place *in* time, and therefore are not necessarily "temporal" (*zeitlich*), such as truth or falsity, are nonetheless "determined by time" (*temporal*), in a sense which, admittedly, remains to be clarified, since with respect to temporal determinations there prevails the greatest confusion in philosophy (GA 21, 199–200).

We can see, then, how the initial ontological question meets that of time, facticity, and historicality; the question which bears on Being as presence turns into the question which bears on the Temporal character of being, and this is how "time became questionable in the same way as Being" (HPT, xii), precisely because of the impossibility of thinking the relation of Being and time on the basis of the traditional concept of time. The initial question of philosophy—posed by Aristotle as *ti to on*, "What is Being?"—thus becomes, insofar as the history of thought summons us to pose it anew, the basis for Heidegger's question of the Temporal meaning of Being that he claims is *phenomenological*, though, to be sure, in a sense different from Husserlian phenomenology of consciousness. Heidegger can then assert in 1969 (QIV, 194), "My question on time was determined on the basis of the question of Being": on the basis of the question of *Being* and precisely not on the basis of a reflection on *consciousness* and its internal temporality. This is why he emphasized that his question was foreign to Husserl's problematics of an internal consciousness of time.

One should not think that, because Heidegger accepted Husserl's request to edit the latter's *Lectures on Internal Time-Consciousness*, which would appear in April 1928, he recognized an influence of the Husserlian thinking of time on his own thought. Certainly Heidegger realized the progress that Husserl's research represented with respect to psychology and contemporary epistemology (BT, 484/432, note xxx); namely, the essential merit of the *Lectures* with respect to the *Logical Investigations* resides in the deepening of the elaboration of intentionality—yet, with respect to time, Husserl continues to see it as something immanent or internal to the subject, while for Heidegger the issue is instead to think the "subject" itself as time. This is why, in the summer semester course of 1928, devoted to the *Metaphysical Foundations of Logic*, which treats of the problem of ground and of the principle of reason (also treated in the small essay *The Essence of Reasons*, written at the same time and dedicated in 1929 to Husserl for his seventieth birthday), Heidegger declares: "That which Husserl still calls time-consciousness, i.e., consciousness of time, is precisely time, itself, in the primordial sense" (MFL, 204/264). Indeed, for Heidegger, there is not, on the one hand, time *itself* in its flux and, on the other, the *modalities* of consciousness through which this flux would be apprehended; rather, there is a single process of *temporalization* which can be given no separate subsistence and, for that reason, eludes all conceptual grasp.

The question of Being and the question of time therefore do not represent two separate themes of Heidegger's thought: the "novelty" of *Being and Time*, on the contrary, consists precisely in having made of these two traditional problems a *single* question, that of the Temporality of Being. Heidegger emphasizes this at the end of *Kant and the Problem of Metaphysics* (which, according to the very terms that Heidegger uses in the preface to the first edition of 1929, "serves as a 'historical' introduction of sorts to clarify the problematic treated in the first half of *Being and Time*"), when he asserts that "the 'and' in this title conceals within itself the central problem" (KPM, 165).

c) THE TEMPORAL MEANING OF BEING

In order to understand the central problem of *Being and Time*, one must turn to the first pages of that book (epigraph and introduction), which we can legitimately assume Heidegger wrote, as he himself said (TB, 80), during the winter semester 1925–26, when he had to think about delivering for publication the results of his research since 1923, in order to be named successor to Nicolai Hartmann in Marburg. Now, the quotation of Plato's *Sophist* that opens *Being and Time* is not, as Heidegger will stress later (KPM, 163), mere ornamentation but instead the indication that the question of the meaning of Being was already posed by ancient metaphysics, which knew something resembling a *gigantomakhia peri tēs ousias*, a struggle between giants about Being (*Sophist*, 246a). For Parmenides and his disciples, the term "Being" was something "quite familiar," and it is Plato himself who speaks in the voice of the Eleatic Stranger when the latter affirms, "we, who formely imagined we knew, are now at a loss" (244a). As long as he remained faithful to the Parmenidean thesis of the radical opposition between Being and non-Being, Plato thought he understood what "being" [*étant*] meant: but he was in a quandary for he found himself obliged to refute the "paternal" thesis and attribute Being to non-Being in order to account for the existence of the sophist. With respect to the entire metaphysical tradition, Heidegger finds himself in the same situation as Plato with respect to Parmenides: for him, too, the issue is to raise again, in a more radical way, the same ancient question which is the *guiding question* of Greek thought, that is, the question of Being. This explains why Heidegger always stressed the fact that *Being and Time* is not a "novelty," for what matters in philosophy is not to say something new, but rather to understand the ancient in a more radical way and to attempt to appropriate it (GA 61, 193; BT, 40/ 19, and GA 31, 115).

But, what does "raising anew the question of Being" (BT, 19/1) mean? Not to take up again the Platonic questioning, but to raise again the same question of the *meaning* of Being, in a way which is even more radical than Plato did, which implies that what is at issue is no longer *beings* but the *Being* of beings. Indeed, Plato's question, like that of Aristotle, bears on the meaning of beings—*to on*—whereas Heidegger's question concerns that which determines all beings as beings, and as *Being* of beings is therefore not itself a being. To be sure, Plato was the one who took the first steps toward understanding the problem of Being, when in the *Sophist* (242c) he asserts that philosophy begins when one stops "telling a story," that is to say defining entities by recourse to some other entities, as is done in the presocratic doctrines of Being (BT, 26/6). Yet, this was already Thales' intention: his question aimed at entities *as* entities, but in his answer he clarified entities on the basis of another entity, namely, water (BP, 319/453). He was also explaining Being on the basis of ontical determinations, which is the common feature of both myth and theology to the extent that the latter has recourse to a God conceived as a supreme being to account for beings in their totality.

Plato and Aristotle had tried to break with precisely such a mode of thought, meaning by the word "philosophy" a science of beings *as such*, whose object would be beings from the point of view of their *essence*. But philosophy defined in this way is still no more than, to use a vocabulary later than that of *Being and Time*, a science of *beingness* (*Seiendheit*) (cf. GA 31, 50). This shows that it still does not move in the dimension of what Heidegger calls the "ontological difference" that constitutes his fundamental thought. The ontological difference will only become thematic in the course of the summer semester of 1927, *The Basic Problems of Phenomenology* (BP, paragraph 22), and in *The Essence of Reasons*, which appeared in 1929 (ER, 27). But the difference between Being and beings already constitutes the implicit horizon of *Being and Time*, in which it is stated several times in the introduction that "Being cannot indeed be conceived as an entity" (BT, 23/4; also 25–26/6 and 62/38). Questioning Being *as such*, indeed, does not mean questioning what is common to all that is, even if, as for Aristotle, one understands the unity of this commonality as analogical rather than generic (BT, 22/3). Rather, it means questioning what constitutes beings as beings, what is the condition of possibility of beings and consequently of a science of beingness. Only that which cannot be said to "be"—only an entity *is*, whereas *there is* Being (BT, 255/212, 272/230, 364/ 316; BP, 10/13)—has a universality still higher than that of what scholastic thought called "transcendentals," that is, the attributes pertaining to all beings. Being as such is not *one* of the transcendentals—next to *unum, bonum, verum,* etc.—but *the transcendens* pure and simple (BT, 62/38), namely, that dimension which is beyond all ontical determination and which the 1943 postscript to the 1929 inaugural lecture, "What Is Metaphysics?" will explicitly understand as "the purely 'Other' than everything that is" (EDS, 256), that is, as nothingness.

According to its Preface, the ambition of *Being and Time* is "to work out the question of the meaning of *Being* and to do so concretely" (BT, 19/1)—of Being thus and no longer simply of beings. Its aim is the "interpretation of time as the possible horizon for any understanding whatsoever of Being." If Heidegger speaks here of a "provisional" goal, it is because he is only referring to the *first* part of *Being and Time*, of which only two of three sections were published in 1927 (see BT, paragraph 8, "Design of the Treatise"). Only the first part, indeed, aims at the interpretation of Being on the basis of time, as its title clearly indicates: "The Interpretation of Dasein in Terms of Temporality, and the Explication of Time as the Transcendental Horizon for the Question of Being." The second part would have treated "The Basic Features of a Phenomenological Destruction of the History of Ontology, with the Problematic of Temporality as Our Clue." Let us clarify immediately that this goal—which is preliminary with respect to the projected "destruction"—which Heidegger had assigned to what should have comprised the first half of the work, was not reached in 1927, since he did not deliver for publication the third division of this first part, entitled "Time and Being." This division alone would have treated "The Explication of Time as Transcendental Horizon of the Question of Being," while the first two divisions ("The Preparatory Fundamental Analysis of Dasein" and "Dasein and Temporality") constitute together "The Interpretation of Dasein in terms of Temporality."

A simple and careful reading of the Preface to *Being and Time* has thus given us an indication of the manner in which the title of the 1927 book should be understood. If, indeed, the goal is to show that time is the horizon which makes possible any understanding of Being whatsoever, whether philosophical or pre-philosophical, then it is not possible to understand the "and" linking Being and time in the sense of an opposition—as is the case in the traditional statement "Being and Becoming." On the contrary, one should take it in the sense of an intrinsic relation between Being and time, something which is only thinkable if the traditional determination of Being as beingness and that of time as a sequence of now-points is replaced by a more original thought of Being and time, capable of bringing out what Heidegger himself called, in his course of the summer semester 1930, their "inner co-belonging" (GA 31, 118).

It is in the Introduction that this co-belonging is clarified. Indeed, the goal of the Introduction, which consists in the "Exposition of the Question of the Meaning of Being," is to awaken anew an understanding for the meaning of the question of Being in an era—dominated by neo-Kantianism, neo-positivism, philosophies of life and phenomenology—which holds any ontology to be impossible. In the second part of the Introduction (paragraphs 5 and 6), Heidegger presents the two tasks required for the elaboration of the question of Being, which correspond to the two parts of the projected treatise. The Introduction, then, anticipates to a great extent the content of the unfinished work published in 1927, and adumbrates the characteristics of the whole problematic elaborated by Heidegger. Thus Heidegger claims (BT, 39/17) that "whenever Dasein tacitly understands and interprets something like Being, it does so with *time* as its standpoint," which implies that all ontology operates unknowingly in the horizon of time even when it opposes Being and Becoming, as in the case of classical ontology. Now, in order to apprehend time as the domain within which all (pre-philosophical) understanding of Being as well all (philosophical) interpretation of Being remain, "*time* needs to be *explicated primordially as the horizon for the understanding of Being, and in terms of temporality as the Being of Dasein, which understands Being*" (ibid.). This explication would have been the topic of the unpublished third division, entitled "time and Being." As Heidegger claimed above, the analytic of Dasein (and the explication of temporality as that which constitutes the meaning of its Being) prepares the ground on which it becomes possible to answer the question of the meaning of Being. *Time* can appear as that which constitutes the meaning of the Being of the entity that is not Dasein (to which, however, Dasein always relates) only on the basis of *temporality* as the meaning of the Being of Dasein. It is striking to note that even in its ordinary sense time is used as a criterion for discriminating various realms of entities. For example, the temporal is distinguished from the non-temporal (the spatial), the a-temporal (the ideal), and the supratemporal (the eternal); the temporal is in each case understood as that which is *in* time. No one has ever questioned the fact that time as such has an ontological function, while for Heidegger what is at stake is precisely to show that "*the central problematic of all ontology is rooted in the phenomenon of time, if rightly seen and rightly explained*" (BT, 40/18).

The content of the third division is thus clearly defined; after having shown that time is the horizon of any understanding of Being, it will be a question of showing in turn that Being is understood *on the basis* of time. This means nothing less than making Being itself visible in its "temporal" or rather "Temporal" character, since what matters is to indicate the *positive* relation that *all* modes of Being entertain with time, which is also the case for the so-called non- or supra-temporal beings (BT, 40/18). Therefore, a Temporality (*Temporalität*) belongs to all modes of Being, and can therefore be characterized as "*horizonal*" in the sense that these modes are understood in the horizon of time, whereas a temporality (*Zeitlichkeit*) belongs to Dasein, which has an understanding of Being, one that is certainly not a pure *intratemporality* but is nevertheless distinguished from the horizonal Temporality of Being by its *ec-*

static character (BT, paragraph 65). It is thus a question of indicating, by virtue of a terminological distinction, the difference between the relation that Dasein, on the one hand, and the entity which is not Dasein, on the other hand, have with time. But this difference is in no way an opposition; ecstasis and horizon are, as will see, inseparable terms, and it is precisely on the basis of their correlation that the relation of time and Being is to be understood.

The concrete answer to the question of the meaning of Being can thus only be found in the exposition of the problematic of Temporality. This answer will become the guiding thread of the ontological inquiry that Heidegger planned to undertake in Part Two of *Being and Time*, and which was to include three divisions, bearing respectively on Kant, Descartes, and Aristotle, which were, for Heidegger, the decisive moments of the history of ontology (BT, paragraph 8). Its purpose was "to *destroy* the traditional content of ancient ontology until we arrive at those primordial experiences in which we achieved our first ways of determining the nature of Being—the ways which have guided us ever since" (BT, 44/22). This destruction is therefore less a shaking off or a reversal of the ontological tradition than the manifestation of the origin of its basic concepts and the delineation of its limits. The regressive path of the "destruction" thus leads from Kant, who expressly referred the interpretation of Being to time, back to Descartes, to whom he remained indebted. The Cartesian moment is characterized by the neglect of an ontological analysis of the subjectivity of the subject, a neglect that itself arises from the absence of a critical debate with ancient ontology, which was transmitted to Descartes through medieval Scholasticism. It would thus be an issue, in that decisive third moment, of showing the meaning and limits of ancient ontology itself in the light of the problematic of Temporality.

Indeed, ancient ontology, too, understood Being on the basis of time, but without an explicit knowledge of the fundamental ontological function of time. On the contrary, it considered time as an entity among others, as is apparent in the very beginning of the Aristotelian treatise on time (*Physics* IV, chap. 10); even before determining the nature of time, Aristotle wondered whether or not time is part of Being. According to Heidegger, this first detailed interpretation of the phenomenon of time has remained determinant for all subsequent accounts of time (BT, 48–49/26). However, one can find evidence that the Greeks unknowingly understood Being on the basis of time in their determination of Being as *parousia* or *ousia* (BT, 47/25). *Ousia* is indeed the fundamental term that, for Plato and Aristotle, designates the Being of beings understood as beingness. In a course following *Being and Time* (the 1930 summer course, *Vom Wesen der menschlichen Freiheit*), Heidegger analyzed the polysemy of this term in detail (GA 31, 45ff). In common usage, this term meant a dwelling place, estate, or property, that is, something constantly available, constantly *present*. The technical usage of the term in philosophical language, that is, as the name for the Being of beings, was made possible on the basis of this fundamental signification. The Temporal meaning of *ousia*, a meaning that remained hidden to Plato and Aristotle themselves, is that of "constant presence." On the basis of this hidden meaning, one can see how *ousia* was used to form the terms *parousia* (presence) and *apousia* (absence). Heidegger claims that *parousia* simply clarifies the meaning of *ousia* (GA 31 61–65), thereby revealing its properly Temporal meaning.

The Temporal-ontological meaning of *ousia* is therefore "presence" (*Anwesenheit*), which signifies that the Being of beings is understood in relation to a definite mode of time, the present (*Gegenwart*). What is the reason for this privilege given to the present? Heidegger answers that it comes from the "guiding thread" chosen by Greek ontology. All ontology requires an access to Being. Philosophical and pre-philosophical Greek thought defined man as a *zōon logon ekhon*, a living being that possesses speech. The emphasis placed on *logos* as the proper dimension of humanity explains why Plato called philosophy, that is ontology, dialectic, which he understood in the *Sophist*—a dialogue to which Heidegger devoted his 1924–25 winter semester course (GA 19)—as the discussion of the relations between the highest genera. If, with Aristotle, dialectic became superfluous, it was not because he no longer understood it but, on the contrary, because he saw its limits. *Legein* is indeed not the sole guiding thread of ontology; *noein*—that is, the pure apprehension of what is already present, and in which Aristotle, as we saw, located truth—is the most simple mode of access to Being, one which Parmenides had already made the guiding thread of his interpretation of Being in Fragment 3 of his poem, . . . *to gar auto noein estin te kai einai*, "for thinking and Being are the same." Now, *legein* and *noein* have the same Temporal structure, that of a pure "presentation" of something that reveals itself through them. This is why the entity that appears in the light of *logos* or of *noesis* can only be conceived as presence, that is, as *ousia*.

It is therefore this Temporal meaning of Being, which runs through the entire history of ontology, that "destruction"—which should be understood, as Heidegger himself stressed, in the sense of a "de-constructing" (BP, 23/31)— seeks to bring to light. This is why, at the end of paragraph 6 of the Introduction, Heidegger wrote: "The question of Being does not achieve its true concreteness until we have carried through the process of destroying the ontological tradition" (BT, 49/26). The answer to the question of the meaning of Being in the first division—namely, that this meaning is Temporal—would allow Heidegger to show in the second division that time itself constitutes the origin of the history of ontology. What becomes clear, then, is the sense in which Heidegger spoke of a "repetition of the question of Being" (cf. BT, title of paragraph 1). Indeed, to repeat involves "raising anew"—that is, more radically—the *same* question. It is in this vein that Heidegger wrote, in the 1930 summer course already cited:

The guiding question: what are beings? must necessarily be transformed into the basic question which enquires about the "and" of Being and time, and thus about the basis for *each of them*. The basic question is formulated as follows: *What is the essence of time such that Being is grounded upon it and that in such an horizon the question of Being, as guiding problem of metaphysics, can and must necessarily be elaborated?* (GA 31, 116)

The transformation of the guiding question of philosophy into Heidegger's basic question is determined solely by the unfolding of its *questionableness— Fraglichkeit*. To fully unfold the guiding question requires an interrogation of the formal structure of all questions as well as of the mode of Being of the entity who questions (cf. BT, paragraph 2). This is how the guiding question, for a thought that only sees man as one entity among others, becomes a *basic* question, for a thought that questions the *basis* for the possibility of the understanding of Being; time, as such a basis, makes both what is questioned (Being) and the one who questions (man) possible. The question of the essence of man then becomes "unavoidable" insofar as it is always included in that of Being (GA 31, 125). The problem of the interpretation of the Being of beings is thus no longer posed on the basis of a unilateral orientation toward beings which are pre-given, which Heidegger calls *Vorhandenheit*: rather, it includes an inquiry into the event of givenness itself (into the "giving" of the *es gibt Sein*) that only occurs with the *opening* of human *existence*. The interpretation of Being thus necessarily implies the analytic of Dasein.

2

◆

The Temporality of Dasein and the Finitude of Time

The all-embracing amplitude of Being is one and the same as the offensive individuation of time

—GA 31, 130

Heidegger's question—the question of the *meaning* of Being—has therefore nothing in common with the traditional ontological question, because it requires the following precondition: the analysis of the Being of the "exemplary" entity that Heidegger calls Dasein (BT, 26/7). Its "exemplary character" resides in its distinction from other entities insofar as it has a relation to its own Being and, therefore, an understanding of Being. It is in this way an ontological entity or, rather (if one stresses the implicit character of this understanding of Being, first experienced before being thematized), a pre-ontological entity (BT, 32/12). The term German philosophy has used since Kant to translate the Latin *existentia*—Dasein: literally "Being-there"—is now used to name the essence of that entity which, because it has an understanding of Being, can only be defined in the mode of possibility, as *existence*. This term, which should be taken in its literal sense (to stand outside of, to rise up, to appear), no longer designates the simple fact of being for any entity whatsoever, but rather only the mode of Being proper to Dasein. The actual understanding that Dasein has of itself is therefore an *existentiell* understanding. But that which, on the other hand, Heidegger names the *existential* analysis is not situated at the simply "ontical" level of concrete individual behavior, but at that of the thematic interpretation of its ontological structure. The task of the *existential analytic* consists in distinguishing and analyzing Dasein's fundamental modalities of Being, its *existentialia*. The difference between the existentiell and the existential, one often neglected by the first readers of *Being and Time*, and which lies at the basis of the existentialist misunderstanding, has to be emphasized. Certainly

17

there is no existential level without an existentiell basis, that is, without the understanding that each particular Dasein has of its own existence. But the existential analysis is not simply directed at one particular entity among others; rather, it concerns an entity which, because it has an understanding of its own Being, also has an understanding of the Being of the entities it is not—an entity which, as Aristotle said of the soul, "is, in a certain way, entities" (BT, 34/14). Because the existential analytic concerns this "pre-ontological" entity, which is the condition of possibility of all thematic ontology, it constitutes the *fundamental ontology* that is the basis of all regional ontologies that have to elucidate the mode of Being of the entities other than Dasein, for example, those that belong to such regions as "nature," "life," "space," and so on. (BT, 33–34/13). The question of Being understood in this sense, far from being a mere speculation dealing with the most abstract generalities, is on the contrary the most concrete question because it is nothing other than "the radicalization of an essential tendency-of-Being which belongs to Dasein itself—the pre-ontological understanding of Being" (BT, 35/15).

However, it remains to be understood why neither Greek ontology nor modern ontologies developed, as a necessary prerequisite, an "ontology of Dasein." How is it that Dasein failed to recognize itself as the condition of possibility of all ontology? Heidegger answers this implicit question by showing that Dasein, while ontically nearest to us, is nevertheless ontologically the farthest. For, if Dasein is indeed capable of understanding itself, it also has a tendency to misunderstand itself as Dasein by understanding itself on the basis of entities that it is not, and with which it is constantly involved; Dasein's understanding of the world is reflected (in the optical sense of the term) back onto Dasein's understanding of itself. However rich the various extant interpretations of Dasein may be—whether psychological, anthropological, ethical, political, historical, and so forth—none of these existentiell interpretations account for the *existentiality* of Dasein or for what distinguishes Dasein from all other entities. Dasein has the "natural" tendency to understand its difference from other entities as merely ontical, rather than ontological. Because Dasein understands itself in terms of "natural" entities, the specific constitution of its Being remains concealed from it. The issue for Heidegger was thus to elaborate anew an analysis of Dasein which, because it would be undertaken with an explicit orientation toward the question of Being, would provide an existential justification to the already extant interpretations. But the existential analysis should not impose any preestablished "interpretation"; it must on the contrary let Dasein show itself from itself in its *average everydayness*, that is, as it exists *proximally and for the most part*. It is therefore the *factical* existence of Dasein that needs to be analyzed, without starting from a presupposed essence or a predelineated ideal of Dasein.

Yet, it is important to remember the goal of this analysis, which is only *preliminary*; it is undertaken in view of the elaboration of the question of Being as such, which is not the same as that of the Being of Dasein. This is why this analysis does not constitute a complete ontology of Dasein and is incapable of providing a sufficient basis for a philosophical anthropology (although the project of a philosophical anthropology could draw a few of its essential items from the existential analysis). In limiting itself to exposing the Being of Dasein without yet interpreting its meaning—this is the object of the first division, "Preparatory Fundamental Analysis of Dasein"—the existential analysis prepares "the horizon for the most primordial way of interpreting Being" (BT, 38/17). This horizon can only be provided through a more primordial interpretation of the Being of Dasein, one which consists in determining the ontological meaning of what the first division had identified as the Being of Dasein (namely, *Care*), as temporality. This is what takes place in the third chapter of the second division, itself entitled "Dasein and Temporality." Temporality is presented in paragraph 65 as constituting the meaning of care. On this properly ontological basis, it becomes possible to repeat the preparatory analysis; this repetition is the subject of the fourth chapter of the second division ("Temporality and Everydayness"), which makes explicit the temporal meaning of the existentialia laid bare in the first division. Yet, this repetition of the first division in the second—interpreting the existentialia as modes of temporality—does not constitute the answer to the guiding question of the meaning of Being, but simply provides the basis on which such an answer could be found. This was to have been the task of the third division, as its title "Time and Being" clearly indicates, since, in contrast to the two preceding divisions, it makes no reference to Dasein. It is quite apparent, simply by reading §5 of the Introduction, that the published part of *Being and Time* does not provide an answer to the guiding question of the meaning of Being. As an interpretation of Dasein through temporality, it only constitutes *one way* toward the *goal*, as Heidegger himself admitted in the last paragraph of the 1927 text (BT, 487/436). We must now follow this way before returning to the crucial question of the incompleteness of *Being and Time*.

a) THE INTERPRETATION OF DASEIN AS CARE

The existential analysis reaches its goal in §65 of *Being and Time*, in which Heidegger interprets the ontological meaning of the being of Dasein as temporality. Before reaching this point, one needs to pause at a crucial juncture, in paragraph 41, where the preparatory existential analysis also reached its goal, namely, the determination of the existential meaning of the fundamental structure of Dasein as Care. The first division is concerned with reaching a "synthetic" interpretation that would unify the existentialia distinguished in the analysis. This is why paragraph 39, which opens the sixth and last chapter of this division, bears on "The Question of the Primordial Totality of Dasein's

Structural Whole." It is indeed necessary to manifest the unitary phenomenon which lies at the basis of the plurality of structural items revealed by the analysis. As in the case of the transcendental analytic (explicitly understood by Kant as the "dissection of the very faculty of understanding," designed to reveal the "connectedness in a system" of the concepts which constitute it), the existential analysis should not be understood as a dissolution into simple elements, but, on the contrary, as the articulation of a structural unity (Z, 150). The question of the unity of Dasein nevertheless remains difficult, for all the traditional concepts of totality are modeled after intra-worldly things and consequently cannot be applied to Dasein. This is the case, for instance, of the concept of a composed totality, or *totum syntheticum*, which presupposes an independence of the parts in relation to the whole and conceives the process of totalization as an assemblage through the construction of elements. One can see, then, why an interpretation that attempts to conceive the whole cannot be a mere recapitulation; in order to reach the whole, we need, on the contrary, to "look all the way *through* this whole to *a single* primordially unitary phenomenon which is already in this whole in such a way that it provides the ontological foundation for each structural item in its structural possibility" (BT, 226/181). This unitary phenomenon, however, is not an *arkhē*, or an origin, that would enjoy the simplicity and uniqueness of an ultimate structural element (BT, 383/334), a foundation in which the manifold would come to disappear. Far from being excluded, the multiplicity of items is, on the contrary, required by the structural unity of the being of Dasein and by the whole it represents, one which, as an articulated structural whole, cannot be "rent asunder." The ontical models of totality are spatial models of the construction and gathering of independent parts; they presuppose space, or the order of the *partes extra partes*, as a medium of dispersion on the basis of which a gathering is possible. On the contrary, to say that "being-in-the-world is a structure which is primordially and constantly *whole*" (BT, 225/180) indicates that Dasein never loses its "being-a-whole" and that the latter perdures in time because it is not formed of parts but rather of "items," which are inseparable from one another. It appears here quite clearly that, by using the term *structure* to designate that which cannot be understood as a mere arrangement of the parts, Heidegger wants to stress the radically relational (and not substantial) character of the existentialia and their reciprocal interdependency.

These structural items are the fundamental ontological characters of Dasein, that is, the existentialia, namely, existentiality, facticity, and Being-fallen (BT, 235–236/191). These three existential determinations are the result of the analysis of Dasein's everydayness, the basic structure of which is *Being-in-the-world*. This basic structure constitutes the starting point of the existential analysis (BT, 78/53). It is indeed essential that one not confuse Dasein—whose essence lies in its "*to* be," that is, in its existence (BT, 67/42)—with an intra-worldly thing which is *already* given (*vorhanden*). This explains why the world is not external to Dasein, but instead represents one of its constitutive items (BT, 77/52). Now, the unitary phenomenon of being-in-the-world can be viewed from three perspectives that would bring out the three structural items that constitute it:

1) The "in-the-world" is the subject of the third chapter of the first division (the first two chapters introduce the preparatory analysis and its theme: Being-in-the-world): "the worldhood of the world." In this chapter, Heidegger wants to show that the ontical concept of world, which takes it as the sum of entities, does not account for the essential structure of *worldhood*, which is not a determination of the non-human entity but rather a character of Dasein itself (BT, 92–93/64). This ontologico-existential concept of the world can in no way be made intelligible on the basis of "nature" in the modern sense of the term (that is, as an object of natural sciences). One should rather, in order to find access to the problematic of worldhood as such, start from everyday Being-in-the-world and from the interpretation of entities encountered in the environment.

2) The entity which has the mode of Being in the world is everyday Dasein. Dasein does not answer to the question "what?"—a question which only concerns intra-worldly things—but only to the question "who?" Its determination is the subject of the fourth chapter of the first division: "Being-in-the-World as Being-with and Being-One's-Self. The They."

3) "Being-in" is the constitutive item of Dasein's relation to the world. It is treated in the fifth chapter of the first division, entitled "Being-in as such," which is composed of two parts:

A) the existential constitution of the There;
B) the everyday Being of the There and the Falling of Dasein.

Dasein is therefore its "there," that is, its disclosedness, on two levels: its primordial existential constitution and its everyday mode of Being. The first level includes the analysis of three existentialia, or three equiprimordially constitutive ways of Dasein, insofar as Dasein is its *disclosedness*: Disposition,[1] Understanding, and Discourse. The second level, which treats of the existential characteristics of the disclosedness of everyday Dasein, considers the *fallen* mode of discourse and understanding in *idle talk*, *curiosity*, and *ambiguity*. Fallenness does not, however, simply concern existentiality, but Dasein's facticity as well, that is to say, its thrownness and disposition. Fallenness is characterized as that specific movement of Dasein through which, "*as long as* it is what it is, Dasein remains in the throw, and is sucked into the turbulence of the 'they's' inauthenticity" (BT, 223/179).

As for the sixth and last chapter of the first division, it is devoted to that which constitutes the unity of these three items: "Care as Dasein's Being."

The expression "Being-in," like *In-sein* in German, can be understood first in the sense of "Being contained in," which is adequate only to intra-worldly things that are actually contained in one another (the water in the glass or the tree in the forest) but not to Dasein, which is not contained in the world but, rather, has an essential relation with it. One should thus distinguish the categorial meaning of "in," which only applies to intra-worldly entities, from its existential meaning, which does not designate a spatial relation of inclusion but rather has the original sense of the German *in*, which, as Heidegger reminds us, comes from the verb *innan*, that is, "to dwell" (BT, 80/54). This dwelling relation to the world takes place first in everydayness—that is, proximally and for the most part—as a "Being alongside" the world (*Sein bei der Welt*), which should not be understood in the categorial sense of a spatial juxtaposition but in the existential sense of proximity, of the possible contact and encounter of beings. Certainly it is always possible, "within certain limits" and "with some justification," to conceive of Dasein as something which is simply given, simply present-at-hand (*Vorhandenes*), and which, because it is included in space, is also worldless. But this implies that one would abstract from or ignore its existentiality. It is not a question, however, of denying Dasein all spatiality, which would be to treat Dasein as a pure mind that would only have external relations to space. On the other hand, one should not unilaterally situate spatiality at the level of the body—which would be to repeat the difficulties of any conception of man as a being composed of mind and matter, and to understand this composition solely in terms of a spatial juxtaposition—but rather perceive its *existential spatiality*, by understanding Being-in-the-world as the basic constitution of Dasein (BT, 83/56). Heidegger attempts to define Dasein's specific spatiality in the third chapter. Dasein's relation to space is one not of inclusion but of givenness, which should be understood as a giving space which is properly a spacing or making room (*Einräumen*) (BT, 146/111, trans. modified). This "spacing" is an existentiale of Dasein, which demonstrates that existence is as much spatial as temporal. This does not mean, however, that space is a form through which the "subject" would apprehend the world, which would presuppose a substantial difference between the subject and the world. It is, on the contrary, as Being-in-the-world that Dasein "gives" or "makes" space; it is spatial because it is in-the-world, and not in the world because it is spatial. It is thus clear, from the existential point of view, that "unless we go back to the world, space cannot be conceived" (BT, 148/113), whereas for classical thought, which only sees the world as the sum of actual things, as the totality of beings—and not as an existentiale—the world is conceived of on the basis of space.

If Dasein is just as much "spatializing" as "temporalizing," then the question of its unity arises even more urgently. We saw that this unity of Dasein cannot be sought in a "synthesis" which is external to the elements it gathers, but rather must be found in a mode of being of Dasein itself. Now, the analysis of everyday Being-in-the-world only presents us with Dasein insofar as it exists in the modality of *dispersion*: the Self of everyday Dasein is the they-self (*Man-selbst*), which must be distinguished from the Self that has taken hold of itself authentically (BT, 167/129). That which answers to the question "who?" at the level of everyday concern—which is characterized by an absorption in the world—is not this or that definite Dasein, but rather the neutral or the They, which represents the primordial phenomenon on the basis of which each Dasein must first find itself. It is therefore not at the level of everydayness that the dispersed Dasein would be able to find its unity, since at that level Dasein is not *properly* or *authentically* itself. Dasein, indeed, *can* be itself, either authentically (*Eigentlichkeit*) or inauthentically (*Uneigentlichkeit*), because it *is* its possibility and must appropriate its own Being (BT, 68/43). The terminologically strict choice of the expressions *Eigentlichkeit-Uneigentlichkeit*, usually rendered by authenticity-inauthenticity, does not imply, however, any moral connotation. On this point, one should recall that the origin of this terminology—something which is either forgotten or not known—is to be found in the *Logical Investigations* of Husserl, who himself found the distinction between the authentic mode of intuitive thought and the inauthentic mode of symbolic thought in the work of his master Brentano (see the footnote on page 236 [215] of *Philosophy of Arithmetics*, as well as Chapter VIII of the Sixth Logical Investigation). This latter text—which for Heidegger represents the height of Husserlian phenomenology—demonstrates how the "empty" intentionality of symbolic thought, which largely represents our way of thinking, can be fulfilled by an intuition, becoming thereby an "authentic" thought. Transposed to Dasein as a whole, this distinction accounts for the non-substantial character of Dasein as well as for its "mineness." Proximally and for the most part, Dasein is a dispersed self. Authentic Being-one's-Self, however, "does not rest upon an exceptional condition of the subject, a condition that has been detached from the 'they'; *it is rather an existentiell modification of the 'they'—of the 'they' as an essential existentiale*" (BT, 168/130). To speak in terms of modification implies, to borrow again from Husserl's phenomenology, that there are not two substantially different "subjects"—the They and the "authentic" self—but rather two different ways of Being the *same* subject (or, as Husserl would say, two different intentionalities toward the same object).

What characterizes this inauthentic Being-a-Self in everydayness is an existentiale that Heidegger names *Verfallen*, Falling, which should not be understood in a pejorative sense, for it does not mean that Dasein falls from a purer, higher, or more primordial level, but is simply the ordinary state of concernful Dasein's absorption in and identification with the world. This Fallenness into the "world," *Verfallenheit an die "Welt"* (BT, 220/175; the quotation marks indicate that in everyday concern the world is taken as the sum of entities and not as an existentiale), does not in any sense mean that Dasein falls out of its essence, but that, on the contrary, it realizes eminently its Being-in-the-world; in everydayness, the not-Being-authentically-one's-self represents a positive possibility of Dasein. Yet, the fact is that the positive possibility of falling as an absorption in the world rests upon the fleeing of Dasein in the face of itself and its authentic potentiality-for-Being-its-Self (BT, 229/184). Now, it would seem that this phenomenon of fleeing in the face of one's self could not provide a phenomenal basis for seeking that mode of Being in which Dasein brings itself before itself and thus becomes accessible, by way of a certain simplification, as a structural whole (BT, 226/182). But one should not, here, confuse the existentiell with the existential; certainly, from an existentiell point of view, by fleeing Dasein closes itself off as authentic Dasein; but existentially, to be closed off is also a disclosure, in the mode of privation, since Dasein flees *in the face of itself.* To flee in the face of oneself is nevertheless to be confronted with oneself: "That in the face of which Dasein flees, is precisely what Dasein comes up 'behind'" (BT, 229/184). Strictly speaking, Dasein can only flee in the face of itself if it has first been brought before itself. But this confrontation with oneself is neither perceived nor understood, only *felt,* for it is fear that provokes the fleeing. Not all shrinking back is necessarily a fleeing, but the shrinking back before that which provokes fear has the character of fleeing. The question arises: Can one be afraid of oneself? Heidegger had already analyzed fear (in paragraph 30) as a mode of *Befindlichkeit*—disposition, which is an existential of Dasein as Being-in-the-world—and his choice of that particular mood (fear as opposed to joy or sadness) was certainly not arbitrary. The analysis showed that fear can only be provoked by an intra-worldly entity that draws close from a definite region of the world. On the other hand, in the fleeing that is characteristic of Being-fallen, Dasein flees in the face of itself, and not in the face of an intra-worldly thing. Furthermore, this fleeing has a peculiar feature in that it consists in turning toward the world and absorbing itself in it. It is thus a matter neither of fear nor of apprehension (*Furcht*), but rather of *anxiety* (*Angst*).

Indeed, Heidegger strictly distinguishes these two modes of disposition, which the Christian tradition as a whole rather tended to confuse, although Kierkegaard, that believer, nonetheless went the farthest in the analysis of the phenomenon of anxiety (BT, 235/190). Heidegger recognizes his debt to the Kierkegaardian analyses (not only of anxiety, but also of existence and the moment of vision), while at the same time underlining their limits (BT, 278/235 and 388/338): Kierkegaard, because he is not a thinker but a Christian author—"the only one in accord with the destining belonging to his age" (QCT, 94)—remained within the dimension of faith and therefore at the existentiell level, and thus was unable to reach the properly existential problematic. In his *Concept of Dread,* Kierkegaard concerns himself with the problem of original sin within a theological context. For Heidegger, on the contrary, anxiety refers exclusively to

Being-in-the-world as such and not to a possible Being-outside-of-the-world of Dasein. Anxiety differs from fear by its being absolutely indefinite: that in the face of which one is anxious is no particular intra-worldly entity and does not approach from any definite region of the world, for "that" which makes us anxious is already there, at once nowhere and yet so close that it takes our breath away, literally choking us (*Angst* has the same root as the latin *angustus*, which means narrow). But if, in anxiety, intra-worldly entities as a whole lose all significance, if they no longer present themselves as entities that can be *handled—ein Zuhandenes*—it does not mean that anxiety is the nihilistic experience of the *nihil negativum* but rather the experience of that "something" in the original sense, that is, *the world as such* (BT, 231/187). The world, in everydayness, is never disclosed as such, but can only "announce itself" and "light up" (*aufleuchten*) when concernful dealings—which are never concerned with one particular entity but always with a complex of intra-worldly entities that refer to one another, that is, an ensemble of "equipment"—are disrupted because the equipment proves either unusable, missing, or standing in the way (BT, paragraph 16). In anxiety, on the other hand, the world is primordially and directly disclosed as world. Disposition, as an existentiale, is such that it discloses Dasein to the world as a *whole* more primordially than any theoretical gaze could: disposition is a basic mode of Dasein's *disclosedness* to the world, to its own Being, and to other Dasein. From the existential point of view, disposition includes the constitutive paradox of what Kant called pure sensibility, and about which Heidegger, in his book *Kant and the Problem of Metaphysics*, said that it must be conceived both as receptivity and "creativity" (KPM, 29–30). What characterizes this sensibility is a *"disclosive submission to the world, out of which we can encounter something that matters to us"* (BT, 177/137–138). We thus owe our first encounter with the world to disposition. Far from being merely the "affective" accompaniment of a seeing and a doing, disposition is, on the contrary, that through which we first encounter the world; anxiety is the fundamental mood in which *"the disclosure and the disclosed are existentially selfsame"* (BT, 233/188), because, as mood, it is not only anxiety *before* Being-in-the-world, but also *for* Being-in-the-world as such, and not simply for this or that possibility of Dasein to which the other modes of disposition relate. Anxiety is indeed always anxiety before a *freedom* to which Dasein is at the same time delivered. This is why "anxiety individualizes and isolates Dasein for its ownmost Being-in-the-world" (BT, 232/187, trans. slightly modified).

What is, however, the meaning of this individualization? Heidegger goes so far here as to speak of Dasein in terms of *solus ipse*; yet, he immediately adds that this is an *existential* "solipsism." Anxiety indeed isolates, in the sense that it individualizes, Dasein; it accomplishes that existentiell modification by which the self as the They becomes an "authentic" self. It isolates Dasein, thus, in the sense that it tears Dasein away from its absorption in the world of concern to throw it toward its ownmost Being-in-the-world; it therefore does not cut Dasein off from the world but rather makes Dasein realize that it is bound to it. In anxiety, Dasein does not break with the world, but with the *familiarity* that characterizes everyday Being-in-the-world. It is that link to the world which undergoes a modification: Being-in, which, as we saw, has in everydayness the sense of a dwelling, here takes on the existential mode of the *not-at-home* (*Un-zuhause*), which implies that the experience of not-Being-at-home, the experi-ence of "uncanniness" (*Unheimlichkeit*), is still a way of maintaining an essential relation to the world. This way of Being-in-the-world in the mode of uncanni-ness is, however, from an existential and ontological point of view, "the more primordial phenomenon," on the basis of which something like a Being-in-the-world in the mode of familiarity is possible. The fleeing characteristic of Being-fallen is therefore fleeing *toward* familiarity *before* Dasein's uncanniness, insofar as it is *thrown* into the world. Is anxiety, insofar as it individualizes Dasein by tearing it away from its everyday absorption in the world of concern—by free-ing it from its initial "captivity" through the "revelation" of its own freedom—the sought-after phenomenon that would give Dasein access to its own unity?

To answer this question, one needs to look at the whole phenomenon of anxiety: as a *mood [disposition]*, anxiety is a way of Being-in-the-world; that in the face of which we have anxiety is *thrown* Being-in-the-world; that which we have anxiety about is our *potentiality*-for-Being-in-the-world. The entire phe-nomenon of anxiety thus shows the inseparability of the two existentialia of *thrownness* (*Geworfenheit*) and *projection* (*Entwurf*), which Heidegger calls *facticity* and *existentiality* (BT, 235/191), insofar as these structures of Being-in-the-world are now to be understood as structures of care. Because Dasein is not indifferent to its own Being, because it "understands" it, it *exists* in the mode of the projection of its own Being, it is for the sake of its own potentiality-for-Being, just as, in each of its worldly tasks, Dasein is for itself its own finality—which Heidegger calls the *Worum-willen* (BT, 116/84), literally: the aim of its will. This is why Dasein can be said to be *"ahead"* of itself, always to precede itself as a projection of itself. But this Being-ahead-of-itself concerns Dasein insofar as it is-*already*-in-the-world, already *thrown* into it, and it is this *thrownness* that, in disposition, Dasein proximally and for the most part feels in the mode of a fleeing that turns away (BT, 175/136). Any project, as Heidegger reminds us in the *Letter on Humanism* (BW, 217), is a thrown project; this means that existence is always a factical existence. Furthermore, anxiety reveals that factical existence takes place for the most part and proximally as concern and absorp-tion in the world: *Being-fallen* characterizes the "inauthentic" mode of Being of Dasein. Yet, it is problematic to see Being-fallen included, along with facticity and existentiality, as one of the structures of care (BT, 235/191), when it only characterizes the everyday and "inauthentic" concernful Being-in-the-world. Now, the formula used by Heidegger to explain the Being of Dasein as concern;

"ahead-of-itself-Being-already-in (the world) as Being-alongside (entities encountered in the world)" (BT, 237/192), reveals, with facticity and existentiality,
the item of *Being-alongside—Sein-bei*. Is this identical to falling? Is it not possible to conceive of a concern or a Being-alongside entities (encountered in the
world) that is not necessarily an inauthentic mode of Being for Dasein? Indeed, Dasein's authentic mode of Being, its "authenticity," in no way signifies
a pure relation to oneself taking place outside of the world, but rather another
way of Being-in-the-world. Heidegger makes this point quite clearly when he
stresses that care does not designate an isolated attitude of the I toward itself.
In fact, the two other structural items (Being-already-in . . . and Being-alongside . . .) are always posited together in care (BT, 237/193).

Heidegger calls "care" (*Sorge*) the structure articulating the three basic
existentialia into a unitary phenomenon, but with the intention of stripping
this term of any moral or existentiell connotation in order to seize it only in
its ontological and existential meaning. This terminological choice, however, is
not arbitrary, since it can serve as a "pre-ontological document" that testifies
to the fact that Dasein understands itself away from any theoretical interpretation, that is, as care. Heidegger finds such a document in a poetical work,
more specifically, a fable from Hyginus that was already noticed by Herder
and Goethe, not only because care is considered as that to which man belongs
for his lifetime, but also because it appears in connection with the way of
taking man as a composite of body (earth) and spirit. Besides, the Latin *cura*
has the same double meaning of care and concern contained in the German
Sorge, in which Heidegger sees the *unity* of the essentially *twofold* structure of
the thrown project (BT, 243/199). In light of this pre-ontological document,
the traditional definition of man as *animal rationale* appears non-originary,
since it conceives of man as a composite of sensible and intelligible, as opposed
to a "whole." Indeed, Heidegger attempts to show, in paragraph 41 of *Sein
und Zeit*, that care is ontologically prior to willing, wishing, urge, and addic-
tion, that is, to those drives that one usually considers characteristic of life or
animateness in general. In claiming that Dasein and its care cannot be understood on the basis of a reflection on the properties of life, Heidegger breaks
with the "philosophy of life" that characterized German thought since the
Romantic period. In the process, Heidegger strongly insists that the analysis of
Dasein does not belong to a general biology that would have as subdivisions
anthropology and psychology (BT, 75/49). In 1946, he declares to Jean Beaufret
(BW, 204): "Nor is the error of biologism overcome by adjoining a soul to the
human body, a mind to the soul, and the existentiell to the mind." Biologism
cannot in any way account for that which constitutes the *humanity* of man—
and the very possibility of considering human beings from a racial point of
view is here radically put aside. On the contrary, biology itself is founded on
the ontology of Dasein, which implies that an ontology of life can only be

effectuated through a privative interpretation. Its task would be to determine that which is merely alive on the basis of Dasein's experience of its own existence (BT, 75/50 and 238/194). This is why of "all the beings that are, presumably the most difficult to think about are living creatures." Therefore, man has traditionally been defined as *animal rationale*, in a way which is, however, "still premature" and which ignores the "enigma" (BW, 204–206). It is therefore a question of producing a more original interpretation of the Being of man, in which the latter would be thought of as a "whole" being, not a composite of corporeal body and spiritual form. This unitary phenomenon, accounting for the non-composite character of the Being of man, is, however, not simple: it includes a threefold structure that cannot be reduced to the unity of a first element. This is why Division I ends with the repetition of the same question, that of the "totality" of Dasein.

b) Temporality as Ontological Meaning of Care

The outcome of the fundamental analysis of Dasein is the interpretation of Dasein as care. But is this interpretation primordial? This is the question raised by Heidegger in paragraph 45 which opens Division II, "Dasein and Temporality." His answer is negative. The analysis conducted in Division I does not reach the "authenticity" of Dasein, that is, what is proper to Dasein, for it has remained at the level of average everydayness. It is thus necessary to leave the phenomenal basis of everydayness behind in order to grasp Dasein in its primordiality. One might wonder whether the phenomenon of anxiety does not already provide the required new phenomenal basis, for anxiety does bring Dasein before its ownmost potentiality-of-Being, that is, its being-free. Yet, this does not attest that Dasein effectively seizes its ownmost potentiality-of-Being, and projects its existence on such a basis. On the contrary, for the most part anxiety is not understood as such, and, furthermore, it occasions the fleeing of Dasein in concern. It is thus necessary to find another mode of existence, one in which, with neither lack nor mask, Dasein would exist in the totality of its structures.

Raising the question of the possibility of Dasein's Being-a-whole amounts to facing a formidable difficulty that has already appeared: as long as Dasein exists, it is in the mode of incompleteness, in the sense that something remains constantly outstanding; and when there is nothing left outstanding, there is no more Dasein: this is death. The existential analysis of death intends to solve precisely this aporia, by showing that Dasein entertains a relation with its own end, that it exists as *Being-toward death* and that, in *anticipating* death, Dasein for the first time makes itself understand its own Being-ahead-of-itself, thus making possible its authentic existence. Indeed, death is different from all other possibilities through which Dasein understands itself in everydayness, in that it offers nothing to actualize: "Death, as possibility, gives Dasein nothing to be 'actualized,' nothing which Dasein, as actual, could itself *be*. It is the possibility of the impossibility of every way of comporting oneself toward anything, of every way of existing. In the anticipation of this possibility it becomes 'greater and greater'; that is to say, the possibility reveals itself to be such that it knows no measure at all, no more or less, but signifies the possibility of the measureless impossibility of existence" (BT, 307/262). Death is for Dasein the possibility par excellence, precisely because it offers no goal to actualize, nothing like an actuality. Because of this very non-actuality, the possibility is revealed as such in its truth. It is thus only in the anticipation of death that Dasein is able to experience itself as possibility, potentiality-of-Being, and not as an ontical reality (as it does constantly as fallen). Dasein, then, understands that it does not exist in the mode of something outstanding, which only characterizes ontical realities. This way of understanding oneself as incomplete or unfinished only arises from Dasein's self-understanding in the horizon of concern and in relation to the actuality and actualization which are proper to such an horizon. In the anticipation of death, Dasein experiences the fact that all possibilities of actualization are founded upon the pure possibility of Being-in-the-world, which can never be "actualized" or "realized" (and thus "suppressed"), but rather demands each time to be renewed as possibility. One understands, then, that the unity and totality of existence cannot be understood on the basis of the *sum* of the possibilities of actualization that Dasein gives itself or takes upon itself, for so long as Dasein exists, this sum is indeed incomplete. It is then only on the basis of Dasein's self-understanding in everydayness that it can be said to be incomplete, in the sense that at that level it remains *dispersed*.

However, is there not an actuality of death in the case of the death of the Other? And, in the final analysis, is not the death of the Other the only "reality" that death has for us? To this objection, Heidegger answers that it is always possible to take the place of the Other in the world of concern, a world which is never private, but rather always for everyone, a *Mitwelt*. On the other hand, with respect to death, there is no possibility of substitution. I, indeed, cannot take the Other's dying away from him as I can relieve him from some task by accomplishing it in his place. In everydayness, "one Dasein can and must, within certain limits, '*be*' another Dasein" (BT, 284/240). But death allows no substitution: to die in the place of the Other, that is, to sacrifice oneself in some definite affair, in no way takes the Other's *own* death away from him. Death is not a factual given, but an existential phenomenon which, like existence, is constituted by *Mineness* (BT, 285/241). The biological event of the ending of life concerns that which lives, but that which characterizes Dasein is precisely that its physiological death, or "demise," can never ontically be isolated from Dasein's relation to its own death, which alone Heidegger calls "dying": "Accordingly we must say that Dasein never perishes. Dasein, however, can demise only as long as it is dying" (BT, 291/247). The issue for

Heidegger is to distinguish the existential interpretation of death from an ontology of life, as well as from a metaphysics of death, for the latter, whether in the guise of an ontical speculation on the afterlife or of a theology and theodicy of death, demands an existentiell stand toward it and an assignment of meaning to it that methodologically presuppose the existential analysis (BT, 292/248.)

Dasein, as *Being-toward-death*, can only endure death as the possibility of the measureless impossibility of existence. This does not mean contemplating it, that is, reducing it to the measure of thought, not even merely expecting it in a non-violent tension. Such expecting would still give death an actuality that is yet to come. It is rather an issue of standing before the *imminence* of death, that is, of preserving its character of pure possibility. This becomes possible only in what Heidegger calls the *anticipation* of death, by which Dasein projects itself in advance into the possibility that it is and thus discloses it as the possibility of the closure of Being. Dasein is indeed *open* to itself, to others, and to the world only insofar as the possibility of the closure of everything that is constantly threatens it. Dasein can never become master of this "unsurpassable" possibility. This constitutive structure of existence, which Heidegger calls *disclosedness (Erschlossenheit)*, can be fully understood only in reference to a more primordial closure that does not disappear in and with disclosedness but, on the contrary, remains its imperishable source. This is why, in the anticipation of death as "authentic" relation to death, Dasein understands itself in the entirety of the constitutive items of its disclosedness (BT, 186–7/146), it reaches *transparency* with respect to its own existence. This self-transparency, however, only announces itself as an ontological possibility, that is, it remains a "phantasmagorical claim" as long as this potentiality-of-Being-a-whole has not been ontically attested by the Dasein itself. One could indeed object that this potentiality-of-Being-a-whole is merely an impossible ideal that is imposed on Dasein from the outside, an artificial construction through which Dasein's Being would be deduced on the basis of an a priori idea of man (BT, 226/182). In fact, the sole purpose of the existential analysis is to conceptualize what has already been disclosed at the ontico-existentiell level (BT, 241/196).

Heidegger discovers the testimony by which the existentiell possibility of Dasein's "authentic" potentiality-for-Being is attested in the phenomenon of *conscience (das Gewissen)*. The phenomenon of conscience is not a specific cultural phenomenon—the German *Gewissen* has been used to translate the Greek *syneidēsis*, which in the New Testament designates the knowledge of good and evil—but rather a primordial phenomenon of Dasein that demands a strictly existential analysis, apart from any theological perspective. This requires that the everyday self-interpretation of Dasein is taken into account, for it is at this level that the phenomenon of "the voice of conscience," or the call that rings out within Dasein itself, occurs. This call is radical, constant, and yet silent; it says nothing, gives no definite instruction, but simply summons Dasein to its ownmost potentiality-for-Being. The exterior character of the call does not refer in any way to a calling agent, just as "no one" throws Dasein into existence: the call, like thrownness, pertains to the facticity of existence. The one who is called in the call is Dasein itself as existing in an inauthentic mode, in the mode of the They, and it is called to nothing if not to its ownmost potentiality-for-Being. As for the one that does the calling; it is Dasein itself, which explains why in the phenomenon of the voice of conscience the call comes at the same time from me and yet from beyond and over me (BT, 320/275). We find here once again the same "identity" between agent and patient that characterized the phenomenon of anxiety. In both cases, it is the same Dasein, but in two different modes of Being: hence the uncanniness of the call, which makes it impossible to consider the phenomenon of the voice of conscience as that of a dialogue with oneself (BT, 318/273). The voice of conscience gives itself as foreign because it is that of Dasein in its "uncanniness," that is, "primordial, thrown Being-in-the-World as the 'not-at-home'" (BT, 321/276), already experienced in anxiety. One finds again, in the structure of the call, the threefold structure of care, the meaning of which is temporality: the one who is called is Dasein as fallen, absorbed by the world, and existing in the *present*; the one who calls is Dasein in its pure facticity of Being-in-the-world, the Dasein as thrown, who exists in the mode of the *having-been*; that to which it is called is "authentic" Dasein, which projects itself, as thrown, into the *future*. Because it does not call to *do* this or that, but simply to *be* in another mode, the call has a formal character, just like the Kantian imperative.

Now, the call of conscience gives one to understand Dasein as being-guilty—as *Schuldigsein*. The German term for guilt, *Schuld*, which in the plural also means "debts," has the same root as the verb *sollen*, which signifies obligation. One should not thus understand "guilt" as a lack, for the idea of lack can only apply to something given as present-at-hand: only in the order of things can there be a deficiency or a flaw. Heidegger undertakes a "formalization" of the idea of guilt in order to distinguish it from all those phenomena that apply only improperly to Dasein. There nevertheless remains something "negative" in this idea, which also implies a sense of responsibility: this is why the formal idea of guilt is determined as "being-the-basis of a nullity" (BT, 329/283). This is "guilt" in an existential and not an ethical sense, for it does not arise out of the perpetration of a misdeed but, on the contrary, constitutes the existential condition of possibility of all ontical guilt, as well as of all "moral" interpretations of existence. One should not, however, confuse this primordial existential "guilt" with the Christian theme of sin: the ontology of Dasein "knows in principle nothing about sin," precisely because sin is always understood as a perpetration of a misdeed, including the case of "original sin" (BT, 354/306, note ii). Rather, Heidegger is concerned with showing that all ontical guilt rests upon a more primordial "guilt" and that Being-guilty does not derive from an "original" sin. The Being-guilty of Dasein can only be understood on the basis of its own Being, that is to say, care. The item of Being-thrown means that Dasein did not itself bring itself into existence and that it is, as it were, always late in relation to itself with respect to its own disclosure: it finds itself, in fact, always already disclosed as Being-in-the-world. Such a "facticity" is not an event that has happened once and for all. An existential analysis of birth could show, no less than death, that birth has nothing in common with a datable event; on the contrary, as long as Dasein exists, as in the case of death, birth does not cease to "happen": certainly man comes into the world only once, on the day of his birth, but he comes constantly to Dasein as long as he lives. Heidegger in fact only alludes to this theme (BT, 426/374), but it helps us understand that if one speaks of thrownness in the past tense, it cannot be in the sense of something being past, but instead in the sense in which there is something unretrievable in existence: Dasein does not posit its own basis; it is its own basis existently, that is, in the mode of taking over its own facticity, which is that of a being disclosed to itself and existing for itself. It is this non-mastery of oneself—which is not, however, a pure and simple yielding to facticity, since the latter, on the contrary, demands to be "taken over"— that constitutes the "nullity" of Dasein. This nullity refers not only to thrownness but also to projection itself, insofar as Dasein's Being-free implies that, as it exists in a chosen possibility, Dasein *does not* exist in another possibility which it *could not* choose.

The existential nullity is in no way a lack or privation with regard to an inaccessible ideal; rather, it is a "negativity" that constitutes Dasein itself and lies at the basis of that possibility that Dasein has of *not* being itself authentically in Falling (BT, 331/285). This implies that the "fall" is not a mere "accident," but is rather constitutive of Dasein as such. It is therefore Care itself which is "permeated with nullity through and through," and the call of conscience is nothing other than the call of Care, insofar as the latter is constituted by Being-guilty, which is what is heard in the call. Therefore, Dasein stands together with itself primordially in the uncanniness of the voice that calls (BT, 333/286–287), whereas in falling, Dasein flees itself. The call summons Dasein to its own potentiality-for-Being: it calls Dasein forth to the possibility of taking over, in existing, the thrown entity that it is, and calls Dasein back to its thrownness so as to understand this thrownness as the null basis which it has to take up into existence (BT, 333/287). The call is thus a call not to avoid guilt, but to assume it and thereby to acknowledge it. In understanding the call, Dasein chooses to be authentically what it is, that is, a being-guilty: to understand the call means *"the will to have a conscience"* (BT, 334/288, trans. slightly modified)—the will being understood here as the fact of being ready to be called.

Dasein attests its ownmost potentiality-of-Being in the will-to-have-a-conscience, and thus opens itself to the "authenticity" of its existence. Heidegger names this distinctive mode of disclosedness (*Erschlossenheit*) of Dasein, through which it understands itself on the basis of its ownmost potentiality of Being, *resoluteness* (*Entschlossenheit*): it is the prefix (*Ent-* instead of *Er-*) which marks the passage from the *state* of disclosedness to its assumption. Resoluteness, like disclosedness, is constituted by the three existentialia of understanding, disposition, and discourse, in their authentic mode, that is, as the "*reticent self-projection upon one's ownmost Being-guilty, in which one is ready for anxiety*" (BT, 343/296–297), silence not being the opposite of speech but rather one of its essential modes (BT, 208/164). Resoluteness does not, however, signify the end of the domination of the They and its irresoluteness; instead, it reveals it and remains dependent upon it in the mode of *resistance* (*Widerstand*): it is in remaining *in* the They that resolute Dasein opens itself to the factical possibilities, but it no longer considers them as so many contingent facts and as a preexisting given, and grasps them instead as the *Situation* in which it exists. As resolute, Dasein therefore is already *taking action*, not in the sense of a real action upon the world but in the sense that Dasein *chooses* the factical existent which it is (BT, 347/300). Dasein is therefore resolved to nothing other than to what it already is inauthentically and improperly. This is why resoluteness, as *authentic Being-one's-Self*, in no way detaches Dasein from the world: on the contrary, Dasein finds itself brought authentically alongside entities and into Being with Others, for resoluteness is nothing other than *authentic Being-in-the-world* (BT, 344/298).

Resoluteness attests that the "authenticity" of Dasein is not an empty notion or an idea that someone has fabricated (BT, 348/301). Resolute Dasein actually achieves *authentic* self-*transparency* (BT, 346/299). But this in no way means that it is the master of its own existence. Dasein can only understand itself as disclosedness if it experiences itself as such in the horizon of a more primordial closure, when it understands that *there is* disclosure and *not* only closure; this is not merely a subsidiary remark but represents the very condition of possibility of the understanding of disclosedness as such. Indeed, the issue for Dasein is to understand that it is factically disclosed, but that it might not be and that total closure, that is to say, death as constantly imminent, threatens it as long as it exists. Therefore, Dasein relates not only to the disclosedness that it is but also to the closure that death is. There is, then, only resoluteness in connection with a being that is authentically toward death, which Heidegger has called anticipation, and this is why the two items are joined in *anticipatory resoluteness* to form Dasein's existentielly authentic potentiality-for-Being-a-whole (BT, paragraph 62).

Indeed, resoluteness *in itself* contains, as a possible existentiell modality, Being-toward-death, and it is the possibility of this existentiell modalization that needs to be brought to light. Resoluteness is indeed the will-to-have-a-conscience, insofar as this will "chooses" the will-to-be-guilty, which is understood not as an accidental guilt but as a constant Being-guilty, that is, as that which constitutes the Being of Dasein as long as it is, "right to its end" (BT, 353/305). The "authentic" existentiell assumption of Being-guilty then requires that Dasein open itself to the constitutive nullity of its Being-a-nullity that is at once "native" and "final"—that is, to the *primordial* truth of existence, since Being-guilty is *authentically* and wholly understood for the first time in anticipatory resoluteness (BT, 354/306–307). Resoluteness, therefore, only becomes authentic when it includes the anticipation of death, for it alone reveals Being-guilty on the basis of the whole Being of Dasein. But conversely, anticipation, due to its intrinsic connection with resoluteness, no longer appears as a possibility that someone has fabricated and imposed from the outside on Dasein, but as the possibility of a Being-authentic for Dasein insofar as Dasein has made itself transparent to itself in an existentiell manner in the will-to-have-a-conscience (BT, 357/309).

In bringing to light the intrinsic connection between anticipation and resoluteness, an *existentiell* (and not only existential) solution to the "factical-existentiell" question of the potentiality-of-Being-a-whole of Dasein has been found. This implies that Dasein as a whole is not "given" and that the question of its Being-a-whole is not theoretical: this Being-a-whole has to be "attested," that is, ontically "produced" or "willed." That the potentiality-for-Being-a-whole demands the "involvement" and the "will" of Dasein should not, however, invite us to see in anticipatory resoluteness a subterfuge fabricated in order to overcome death, for it is less a "voluntarism" of "authenticity" that would bring about the annulment of death than it is an understanding of existence that frees for death the possibility of acquiring power over Dasein's existence (BT, 357/310). This "will" is in fact a letting, as Heidegger himself stressed in a 1953 footnote added to his 1935 course, *Introduction to Metaphysics* (IM, 21). Anticipatory resoluteness is no more a fleeing away from "action" than it is an idealistic claim to float freely above existence; rather, it consists in bringing Dasein back into the sober understanding of its factical existence. The ontological interpretation of existence, indeed, acknowledges the *positive* necessity of taking a definite ontical conception of existence as its basis, and of assigning to Dasein a factical ideal, for this does not constitute an ontical limit of ontology, nor a forced consent to some incontestable presuppositions, but rather the very unfolding of Dasein's self-interpretation.

Now, what we experience in anticipatory resoluteness, that is, at the level of what is proper to existence, is temporality as constituting the ontological meaning of care, that is, the Being of Dasein (BT, paragraph 65). Thus, with temporality we have reached the primordial and unitary phenomenon that accounts for all the structures of Dasein, which are all structures of temporality or modes of temporalization of temporality (BT, 351–352/304). The unity of care is indeed a *temporalization* (the German term that Heidegger uses, *Zeitigung*, expresses "the work" of time, *Zeit*, and literally means "maturation"), a unity which is not that of a presence-at-hand that would only be externally framed by time. Indeed, Heidegger is not concerned with taking account of time as a milieu of the *dispersion* of presence. This is why, if he does conceive, with St. Augustine and Husserl, of an equiprimordiality of the three dimensions of time, it is neither in the sense of the threefold presence of the past, future, and present in memory, attention, and expectation (*Confessions*, Book XI), nor in the sense of the unity of protention and retention, the immediate past and future, in Husserl's living present (*Lectures on the Phenomenology of Internal Time Consciousness*). The unification of the dimensions of time effectively continues to occur within a privilege given to the present—the eternal present of God in St. Augustine, which contrasts with the "distention" of the created soul, on the one hand, and the presence-to-itself of consciousness in Husserl, on the other hand, which is capable by itself of overcoming its own dispersion and of gathering itself. Heidegger does not conceive of temporality against the background of an infinite presence-to-self—of God or of that transcendental ego of which Husserl wrote (in a manuscript from August 1936) that it is "immortal"—but as the mode of Being of an existent that is not primordially present to itself but rather has to be or "become what it is" (BT, 186/145), according to the saying borrowed by Nietzsche from Pindar. This explains why the item of existentiality is made to bear all the weight of temporality: it is on the basis of existentiality that the authentic temporality of Dasein temporalizes itself; hence the privilege granted, no longer to the present, but instead to the *future*.

Anticipatory resoluteness, that is, the "authentic" existence of Dasein toward its end (death), presupposes that Dasein is able (to the extent that it *exists* in the mode of *possibility* rather than *is* in the mode of *actuality*) to *come* to itself in general. Understanding itself from its uttermost possibility, that is, death, Dasein is futural, *zukünftig*, that is, coming [*avenant*] or yet to come [*à venir*]. Dasein is *always* futural, whether it understands itself on the basis of its potentiality-for-Being in "authentic" existence or as a present-at-hand reality in "inauthentic" existence. To understand itself as a Being-toward-death means that "authentic" Dasein takes over its Being-guilty, that is, its birth and thrownness. Now, taking over thrownness means nothing other than the fact of being "authentically" what it *already was* "inauthentically." Dasein *can* only be its *having-been* and can only assume its original position by anticipating its end: "anticipation of one's uttermost and ownmost possibility is coming back understandingly to one's ownmost been" (BT, 373/326). Dasein can only be its "past" by returning to it in order to assume it on the basis of the future: "The character of having-been arises, in a certain way, from the future" (BT, 373/326), because there can only be "facticity" for an existence, that is, in the horizon of a potentiality-for-Being. In the authentic sense, the future is not a now that has *not yet* become real but rather Dasein's coming to its ownmost potentiality-for-Being, which occurs in the anticipation of death. Similarly, because Dasein is not an entity that is present-at-hand or given beforehand (*Vorhandenes*), it is never "past" in the strict sense but, on the contrary, has always already been, and remains so as long as it is: the *having-been* (the German says more precisely *Being-been* [*Gewesen-sein*] is the primordial phenomenon that we call the "past." It is thus by *coming-into-Being* in the mode of *coming back* to itself that anticipatory resoluteness makes *present* the entity that it encounters in the environing world: Heidegger calls this unitary phenomenon of a future which makes present in the process of having-been: *temporality* (BT, 372/326).

To summarize: anticipatory resoluteness, as a mode of "authentic" care, is only possible through temporality: this implies that care in general is founded in temporality, which in turn constitutes the ontological meaning of care. It is thus temporality that makes possible the unity of existentiality, facticity, and falling, insofar as they constitute the structural items of care. We can then present the following rough schematic:

Being-ahead-of-itself	as Being-alongside- (the entity encountered within the world)	already-in-(a-world)
Future	Present	Having-Been
Existentiality		Facticity
Projection	Concern-Solicitude	Thrownness
Understanding		Disposition
Being-Toward-Death		Being-Guilty

It is not possible to inscribe the existentialia of falling and discourse in this formal schema, in which the modal difference of "authenticity" and "inauthenticity" does not appear. Discourse, as we will see, temporalizes itself from the present only in its "inauthentic" modality, which is speech. Falling, which constitutes the "inauthentic" modification of the entire structure of care and not a distinct item along with existentiality and facticity, cannot be confused with Being-alongside, which, as a formal structure, must be able to appear "authentically" as well as "inauthentically." We see clearly that, with respect to authentic temporality, the temporal marker contained in the items of existentiality and facticity (the *ahead-of-itself* of projection and the *already* of thrownness, not to be confused with a "not yet" and a "no longer," if we are to avoid identifying care with an intratemporal entity) is missing at the level of the third constitutive item of care, that of Being-alongside the intra-worldly entities. The *making-present* of the intra-worldly entities in which falling is founded does not constitute a *distinct* item at the level of primordial temporality, which, as we saw, challenges the primacy of the present on which the traditional representations of time rest. In "authentic" temporality, the making-present of the intra-worldly entities, that is, the disclosedness of the situation, or "There," of Da-sein occurs in the "moment" of "vision" (*Augen-blick*) and thus remains included in the future and the having-been (BT, 376/328).

Temporality, as the meaning of care, thus makes possible the multiplicity of relational phenomena that characterize the different items of care, as coming *toward* oneself in coming back *to* oneself and being *alongside* the intra-worldly entities: far from constituting the "inner sense" or "interiority" of a "subject," temporality is rather "the *ekstatikon* pure and simple," "the '*outside-of-itself*' in *and for itself*" (BT, 377/329). The term *ekstatikon*—which Heidegger probably discovered in Book IV of Aristotle's *Physics*, where the Stagirite defines the nature of change (13, 222 b 16)—should be taken in its ordinary Greek sense, the fact of stepping outside of oneself, and affiliated with the term existence (BP, 267/377). In calling the future, the having-been, and the present, "ecstases of temporality," it was an issue of emphasizing *temporalization* as a pure movement or event and not the stepping outside of oneself of a "subject" that would first be "in itself." The traditional representations of time all tend to conceive of temporalization in reference to an entity that would function as its substrate or principle, thus giving to time itself a "subsistence," comprised of successive "nows." Far from presupposing the intratemporality of a "subjectivity" or a "self," this "ecstatic" temporality, on the contrary, makes self-constancy, *Selbstständigkeit*, possible (BT, 369–370/323), insofar as this "autonomy" of Dasein is not what escapes time but, rather, that which constitutes it "temporally" and "authentically" as such. But the "constitutive power" of temporality (BT, 380/331)—we note here the persistence of the Husserlian vocabulary of constitution as a means to conceive of that which is not simply subjective or objective—is not, however, unlimited: Dasein is a Being-toward-the-end, which in no way means that in this end it simply ceases to be; on the contrary, Dasein "*exists finitely*" (BT, 378/329). Ecstatic temporality, although it does constitute *primordial time* (in opposition with the traditional conception of time), is nevertheless a finite temporality. This in no way means that time no longer passes when I am no longer there, or that the future does not harbor an unlimited quantity of things, for here the question is not what time harbors, but rather the *way* in which it temporalizes itself. The thesis of a primordial finitude of temporality simply consists in articulating the phenomenal character of primordial temporality that appears as the "thrown projection" that Dasein is, that is, as a potentiality-for-Being whose future is closed and whose basis is "null." It is precisely in order to attempt escaping the finitude of primordial temporality that the ordinary conception of an in-finite time, within which the various finite temporalities would be inscribed, is posited. In the perspective of such a conception, the terms of the problem are inverted, as it were: because the finitude of time is held to be impossible a priori, one asks how the infinite time of generation and corruption can become a finite temporality, instead of asking according to *what mode of temporalization* finite "authentic" temporality becomes an in-finite, "in-authentic" temporality. Indeed, "only because pri-mordial time is *finite* can the 'derived' time temporalize itself as *infinite*" (BT, 379/331). Time *is* not but temporalizes itself: this temporalization is not the result of the succession of temporal "ecstases," but occurs in their *equiprimordiality*. This implies that time is able to temporalize itself in various ways: there are, therefore, different modes of temporalization, depending on whether the prior-ity is given to one ectasis over the other, thus constituting the multiplicity of Dasein's modes of Being and, above all, its "authenticity" and "inauthenticity."

The four theses at the end of paragraph 65 that summarize the analysis of primordial temporality just presented are, therefore, closely connected. As that which makes the constitution of the articulated structure of care possible, time is primordially a *temporalization* of temporality. Temporality, then, cannot re-fer to any subsistence or interiority of a subject, and can only be understood essentially as an *ecstatic* temporality; it *primordially* temporalizes itself from the priority given to the ectasis of the *future*, following the definition of Dasein as potentiality-for-Being. This ecstatic and existential temporality characterizes *primordial time* as *finite*, in contrast with the ordinary understanding of time as an infinite sequence of nows. The "temporal" interpretation of Dasein has thus shown that the ontological constitution of Dasein is only possible on the basis of temporality.

c) THE CONCRETE ELABORATION OF DASEIN'S TEMPORALITY AS
   EVERYDAYNESS, HISTORICALITY, AND WITHIN-TIME-NESS

1) EVERYDAYNESS

In order to show that temporality is the ontological meaning of care—that which renders possible the totality of structures which, in their unity, make up care—it was necessary to consider the *authentic* mode of disclosure of resolute-ness, and consequently to abandon the level of *everydayness* on which the pre-paratory existential analysis had remained up to this point. It is now a question, therefore, of bringing out the *temporal* meaning of the point of departure of the existential analysis that Heidegger had characterized as the "everyday undifferentiated character" of Dasein—undifferentiated with respect to both "authentic" and "inauthentic" modes of Being—which, however, should be understood as the "positive" manner in which Dasein is "proximally and for the most part," and which constitutes its averageness (BT, 69/43). The task thus consists in revealing the specific temporality of the "inauthenticity" of Dasein, which requires the *repetition* of the preparatory existential analysis as a temporal existential analysis.

This in no way means going over the previous analyses and externally im-posing a temporal schema on them, but rather implies articulating them in a different way so as to remove their apparently arbitrary character and to reveal their internal consistency more clearly. There is nothing surprising in the necessity of this repetition, which *refers back* to temporality the essential structures of Dasein's Being that were interpreted *before* the explication of temporality, though in the perspective of leading to it: this is the unavoidable "circular" aspect of an ontology of Dasein, whose presupposition is not an arbitrary principle, but rather an idea of existence drawn from the pre-ontological understanding that Dasein has of itself (BT, 362–3/315). If, indeed, this ontological investigation is itself a mode of the Being of Dasein, which attempts to conceptualize its pre-ontological understanding of Being, then it can only reveal "a remarkable 'relatedness backward or forward' which what we are asking about (Being) bears to the inquiry itself as a mode of Being of an entity" (BT, 28/8). This, moreover, implies that the temporal analysis which repeats the analysis of Dasein remains itself incomplete as long as the idea of Being as such has not been clarified, and that the analysis will have to be repeated in the context of a discussion of the concept of Being (BT, 382/333).

The issue is thus to bring out the *concrete* temporal constitution of care, that is, to interpret temporally each of the structural items of Dasein's disclosure, namely, understanding, disposition, falling and discourse. The three temporal ecstases are constitutive for each of these items, but there is a primary ecstasis for each one: for understanding, the primary ecstasis is the future; for disposition, it is the having been; and for falling and discourse, it is the present. This, however, does not mean that the other ecstases are absent: indeed, each ecstasis is autonomous, in the sense that it cannot be derived from the others, which explains why Heidegger speaks of the *equiprimordiality* of the ecstases. But, as constitutive of the unity of temporality, they are mutually dependent and cannot be isolated. This is why Heidegger explains that "*in every ecstasis, temporality temporalizes itself as a whole*" (BT, 401/350), which implies that all temporalization necessarily involves the three ecstases together. The primary ecstasis simply indicates the direction and meaning [*sens*]² of temporalization. Thus, with respect to understanding, which consists in Dasein's projecting itself in an existentiell possibility, it is the future that constitutes the disclosure of Dasein to itself as a potentiality-of-Being. "Understanding" Dasein is thus constantly *ahead-of-itself*—this is the formal expression designating the future, without yet distinguishing its authentic and inauthentic modes—but it is not constantly in the mode of *anticipation*, which, as we know, is the name for "authentic" future. How then are we to name the inauthentic mode of the future, the "inauthentic" future? What characterizes "inauthenticity" is the fact that Dasein understands itself on the basis of what it is concerned with rather than on the basis of its own finite potentiality-for-Being. Thus "inauthentic" Dasein, with respect to the tasks it performs, understands itself as awaiting itself: *awaiting* (*das Gewärtigen*) is the name for "inauthentic" future. Understanding is primarily determined by the future, but also equiprimordially by the having-been and the present. An inauthentic present corresponds to the inauthentic future, one that is different from the "authentic" Present, *the moment of vision*, which gets held in the future and in having been. Inauthentic present has already been called *enpresenting* or *making present* (*Gegenwärtigen*). As for having been, its authentic mode is the *repetition* by which Dasein, in anticipatory resoluteness, takes over its own Being-thrown, that is, the entity which it already is. On the contrary, when Dasein understands itself from the object of concern, it forgets itself as thrown potentiality-for-Being. This *forgetting* is the "inauthentic" having-been, on the basis of which it is possible to *retain* the intra-worldly entities with which Dasein is concerned, and from which the Dasein lost in the exteriority of concern is able to recapture an interiority in *remembering* itself (the German term *Erinnerung*, which means remembering, literally signifies interiorization). "Inauthentic" understanding, in contrast with the "authentic" understanding as an "anticipation which repeats in the present," can therefore be defined as an "awaiting which forgets and makes present."

The concrete temporal analysis of disposition does not consist in deducing moods from temporality, but simply in showing that their existential signification is only possible on the basis of temporality. Thus the temporal analysis of fear—a mood that has already been used as an example of "inauthentic" disposition—shows that its primordial temporal meaning is not, as it would seem, the future (has not fear been defined as the expectation of some oncoming evil?), but rather having-been, for fear is not so much a fear *in the face of* as it is a fear *about*, and it is this *retroactive effect* of the awaited threat on the being that I am which constitutes the character of fear as affect. But this return to oneself is a forgetting of oneself that manifests itself in the bewilderment which is constitutive of fear and which, unable to take hold of any definite possibility, makes present the first thing that comes into one's head in order to save it. Fear can thus be defined, in accordance with its temporal meaning, as "a forgetting which awaits and makes present," whereas anxiety, as a fundamental disposition, brings Dasein back to its ownmost thrownness as something which can be repeated. Insofar as it is primordially grounded in having-been, anxiety brings Dasein before its possible repeatability; out of this both its future and its present temporalize themselves as the possibility for resoluteness and the moment of vision (BT, 394/343–344).

Falling has its existential meaning in the *present*. The temporal analysis of curiosity alone will suffice for Heidegger to show the primacy of the making-present, which constantly "extricates itself" from awaiting, to the extent that curiosity is characterized by a craving for the new (this is the literal meaning of the German word for curiosity, *Neugier*) that drives to actualize a possibility immediately and to extricate itself from awaiting. That *non-tarrying* which is distinctive of curiosity comes from the ecstatic modification of awaiting, by which the latter no longer constitutes, as it were, the origin but the consequence of the making present, thereby elevated to the level of an end in itself. This mode of the present, which constitutes the possibility of *dispersion*, stands at the opposite extreme from the moment of vision; whereas, in the moment of vision Dasein opens to the situation, that is, takes over its factical possibilities, in the never-dwelling-anywhere that is distinctive of curiosity, Dasein is everywhere and nowhere. However, even in the cases in which the making-present seeks to temporalize itself out of itself, Dasein remains temporal, that is, awaiting and forgetful. Indeed, the basis of falling (the movement by which the present "leaps away" from the future) is "authentic" temporality, or thrown Being-toward-death, which remains closed off from Dasein to the extent that this one gets dragged along in thrownness and loses itself in the world of concern. The present thus represents the existential meaning of the loss of oneself, and closure to oneself, that is constitutive of Dasein's facticity. This loss and closure, however, cannot be total: Dasein would then be of the same kind as the purely present-at-hand Being of "nature." Another ecstatic horizon cannot be reached on the basis of the present itself, since it constitutes the temporal mode of Dasein's closure *to itself*, but only through the disclosure of the "limit-Situation" of Being-toward-death in resoluteness and in the moment of vision (BT, 400/348–349).

The temporal analysis of discourse reveals a *"privileged* constitutive function" of the making-present only to the extent that the facticity of discourse is constituted through language. Discourse as such, that is, as the *articulation* of the disclosedness of the there, does not temporalize itself primarily in any definite ecstasis (BT, 400/349). In fact, although discourse does constitute the third item of disclosedness and, as such, is equiprimordial with understanding and disposition (BT, 203/161), it does not, however, occur independently of them: it is as thrown-projecting that man talks or discourses. This does not necessarily mean that man *speaks*: this is only its oral expression, which Heidegger names speech or language [*Sprache*]. The German *Rede* was chosen by Heidegger to translate the Greek *logos* (BT, 55–56/32), probably because its etymology refers less to the idea of language than to articulation, and because its Latin equivalent is the word *ratio*. *Ratio*, like *logos*, does not designate language— Heidegger notes, "The Greeks had no word for 'language' [*Sprache*]; they understood this phenomenon 'in the first instance' as discourse [*Rede*]" (BT, 209/165)—but its *existential-ontological foundation* (BT, 203/160). This explains why *keeping silent* and *hearing* are said to constitute essential possibilities of discourse. To keep silent has nothing to do with being dumb, and, as a mode of discourse it can make one understand better than words could (BT, 208/164), for the articulation of disclosedness can also take place in the keeping silent. In the same way, we have seen how *"conscience discourses solely and constantly in the mode of keeping silent"* (BT, 318/273). If, thus, the basis for the temporalization of language can be said to be the ecstasis of the "inauthentic" present—since keeping silent constitutes "authentic" discourse—discourse as such is not temporalized in any definite ecstasis, because, as an articulation that manifests beings *as* such and such, it does not reveal a character proper to Being (as does understanding for possibility, or disposition for facticity), but only what Heidegger would later refer to as the *difference* between Being and beings. Discourse can therefore be temporalized either on the basis of the future in "authentic" existence, or on the basis of the present in "inauthentic" existence, for, in both cases the ontological difference—which for Dasein is identical to the very fact of existing—happens (BP, 319/454). However, Heidegger did not see this very clearly in 1927, which explains the terseness of paragraph 68d, which treats of "the temporality of discourse."

On the basis of the temporal analysis of the structures of disclosedness, it becomes possible to determine the temporality of Being-in-the-world, that is, first, the temporality of concern and of its modification in a theoretical comportment toward entities. It is indeed an issue of taking account of the temporal meaning of the *modification* of the understanding of Being through which the meaning of Being as *Zuhandenheit*, or readiness-to-hand (which makes the entity in circumspective concern an entity *for* the hand), changes over to the meaning of Being as *Vorhandenheit*, or pre-sence (which makes the entity in the theoretical gaze something given *before* the hand). Indeed, Heidegger understands *Vorhanden*, which signifies the merely available presence, in the strong sense of what is *already present*, of what is constantly available without prior relation to a particular Dasein (HCT 198–199/270). Concern can be understood in its temporal sense as a *making present that awaits and retains*; awaiting corresponds here to the unthematic understanding of the toward which, of the "finality" of the handling of equipment, and the retention corresponds to the understanding of the with-which that characterizes the essentially instrumental "involvement" of the equipment—what Heidegger designates by *Bewandtnis*, a term difficult to translate—according to which handling never relates to a single equipment but always to a totality of equipment (BT, 96–99/68–69, and 404/353). The concern by which Dasein is absorbed in the world and surrenders to it is therefore not a pure making present, responding to the urgency of everyday necessity, but the mode in which Dasein exists in a world within which it makes intra-worldly entities present on the basis of a retention that awaits. Now, the basis of theoretical comportment is not a pure and simple disappearance of praxis that would lead us to abstract from the instrumental nature of equipment and to simply see in it something merely given, but on the contrary a *new* way of considering it, that is, of understanding its Being. This new way is not merely an "objectification" of entities but also a *delimitation* of the environing world by which the whole of the given (of the *Vorhandenen*) becomes thematic (BT, 414/363). The genesis of the purely theoretical gaze from circumspective concern thus rests on the mathematical projection of nature which sketches, a priori, the plan of nature by way of a modification of the gaze that amounts to depriving the world of its worldhood: from the perspective of temporality, the scientific project as a whole—what Heidegger calls *thematization*—has the sense of a *distinctive kind of making present*, the correlate of which is precisely the pure and simple *pre*-sence (*Vorhandenheit*) of entities that Dasein can only uncover (BT, 414/363).

Both one's Being alongside the ready-to-hand concernfully and one's thematizing of the present-at-hand in the scientific project are made possible by the *transcendence* of the world, which must be already disclosed to Dasein for it to be able, from the *horizons* of the world, to *return* to the entities encountered within them. Indeed, every encounter and every presentation of entities, whether ready-to-hand or present-at-hand, presupposes Dasein's Being-already-in-the-world. Now, the existential-temporal condition of the possibility of the world is the unity of what Heidegger calls the horizonal schemata of the ecstases, that is, what constitutes the "aim" of each ecstatical movement. The world is thus determined as the horizon of the whole of temporality, that is, as that which temporalizes itself unitarily in the outside-of-itself of temporality, and which can only be "there" if Dasein exists. It is on the basis of this temporal transcendence of the world that the temporal meaning of the spatiality proper to Dasein can be understood. This does not mean that space is deduced from time, nor even, in a Kantian sense, that time has a priority over space. It is rather a question of taking account of the independence of space with respect to time, and thus of the possibility of Dasein's breaking into space, that is, Dasein's existence as *making room*. Now, the unfolding of space is only possible against the background of the horizon of the world, from which the enpresenting *bringing-close* of entities occurs equiprimordially with the directional awaiting of a *region* as place of belonging of entities. For, it is not the world that is given in space; rather, it is space that is discovered within the world (BT, 420–421/369).

2) HISTORICALITY

Is it possible, on the basis of the concrete analysis of the temporality of Being-in-the-world, to understand the ontological meaning of the mode of Being in which Dasein remains, proximally and for the most part, and which, under the name of everydayness, has served as a point of departure for the existential analysis? Is it not necessary, in order to account for the *enigma* of Dasein's temporal *stretching* in its day-to-day life, to reconsider the question of Dasein's *Being-a-whole*? Indeed, the existential analysis has so far remained unilaterally oriented toward Being-toward-death and has neglected not only Being-toward-the-beginning, but, above all, Dasein's *stretching along between* birth and death (BT, 425/373). It is now a matter of tackling the problem that Dilthey called the "connectedness of life" (*Zusammenhang des Lebens*), which should not be conceived as an *intratemporal* sequence of Experiences, of which Dasein would be the sum, but as the *ecstatic* stretching-along of the Being of Dasein, who, as care, is the "between" of birth and death (BT, 426/374). The representation of this peculiar stretching of Dasein in terms of spatiality or succession is therefore dismissed here, for that would assume the preexistence of a self which would have the supplemental property of stretching itself. Indeed, the "movement [*Bewegtheit*] of existence is not the motion [*Bewegung*] of something present-at-hand" but the "specific movement in which Dasein *is stretched along and stretches itself along*," which Heidegger calls Dasein's "historizing" (BT, 427/375). As historizing, the Being of Dasein is thus constituted *from the outset* as a stretching along and not as a static self whose relation to time remains problematic, since "as the primary outside-self, temporality is stretch itself" (BP, 270/381).

With the analysis of Dasein's historizing (*Geschehen*) and historicality (*Geschichtlichkeit*), Heidegger returns to a problem already raised in paragraph 64, that of the status of the self and its self-constancy (*Selbst-ständigkeit*). After having elucidated the temporal meaning of Being-in and of the world, there remains to be understood the third item of Being-in-the-world, selfhood, on the basis of time itself (BT, 245/200). The temporal constitution of existence is only achieved through the analysis of historicality. In this chapter, however, it is a question of repeating the existential analysis not as a temporal analysis but as "phenomenological construction" (BT, 427/375). It was only after *Being and Time* (BP, 19–23/26–32) that Heidegger distinguished the three components of the phenomenological method: *reduction*, which he understands as the leading of our vision back from beings to Being, does not constitute the only component of the phenomenological method; it must be supplemented by a *construction*, which consists of bringing Being itself into view. This necessarily implies, for its part, a *destruction*, that is, a critical de-construction of the traditional concepts in order to return to the sources from which they were drawn. The reductive method has thus far guided the existential analysis; but as soon as the meaning of the Being of Dasein has been found in temporality, it is not a question of considering it as the constantly present-at-hand basis of care (BT, 369/322) but rather of showing in what modes ("authentic" or "inauthentic" historicality) Dasein exists as such a basis. This is the meaning of the phenomenological construction of historicality, which, because it "merely reveals what already lies enveloped in the temporalizing of temporality" (BT, 428/376), is just "a more concrete working out of temporality" (BT, 434/382). As such, it serves as a preparation for the destruction of the history of ontology, which the second part of *Being and Time* was supposed to cover by showing that historiology has its roots in the historicality of Dasein (BT, 444/392).

The issue is to emphasize the difference between history as a science or narrative (*Historie*) and the historical "reality" itself, *Geschichte* (from the verb *geschehen*), that is, the totality of the events that can become the object of a scientific thematization. The analysis of what is usually understood by *Geschichte* reveals a distinctive primacy of the past in the determination of what is historical. What, however, is properly historical in a so-called historical object is its belonging to a world which is no longer, but which, as mode of existence of a Dasein having been there, cannot strictly be said to be "past." What is primordially historical, then, is Dasein itself, and the environing world is historical only secondarily. But only at the level of "authentic" existence can the claim that historicality is the essential constitution of Dasein be understood. In anticipatory resoluteness, Dasein understands itself in terms of its finite potentiality-for-Being, and fully assumes its facticity. Dasein does not choose its factical possibilities from death, as that possibility of existence that is not to be outstripped, but rather finds them pre-delineated in the average public interpretation of everyday Dasein's self-interpretation. It is true that, in the anticipation of death, Dasein frees itself from the domination of the They and understands that it has "to take over of itself and from itself its ownmost Being" (BT, 308/ 263–264). But it can do so only as a Being-in-the-world that finds possibilities already given and does not produce them freely. As Being-thrown, Dasein must therefore disclose factical possibilities on the basis of the *heritage* it chooses to take over. It therefore hands *itself* down *to* itself *in* a possibility both inherited and chosen (BT, 435/384). Dasein is thrown into the midst of beings as a free potentiality-for-Being: this is why the *superior power* of its finite freedom (finitude as a projection of Being) can only consist in taking over the *powerlessness* of Dasein's abandonment, a Dasein who is not master of its own freedom (finitude as dependency on a pre-given being).

In fact, Heidegger did more fully develop the problematic of finitude in *Kant and the Problem of Metaphysics* (1929). Finitude, if it is understood in the sense of a dependency on the pre-givenness of beings (a sense which corresponds to the Kantian concept of finitude), is not what is most radically finite in man. Indeed, Kant elaborated this concept of finitude by externally determining it in opposition to an *intuitus originarius*, a productive intuition (GA 25, 410). On the contrary, the "internal" finitude that differentiates Dasein from animals (which are themselves also dependent on something already given) is the *need* of the understanding of Being in which Dasein shows itself *as* Dasein (KPM, 161). It is this transcendental neediness that fundamentally ensures the possibility that there is Da-sein, which helps us understand the statement, "*More original than man is the finitude of the Dasein in him*" (KPM, 156). Finitude, then, is not an accidental property of human reason, nor the mere lack of a creative intuition, but the submittance to the understanding of Being, which implies that "there is and must be something like Being where finitude has come to exist" (KPM, 156). It is thus finitude itself that can make possible the "creative" faculties of man. Heidegger calls this conjunction of Dasein's powerless dependency upon the pre-givenness of beings, and of Dasein's overpowerful submittance to the understanding of Being, *destiny* (BT, 436/385). With freedom toward death, Dasein has reached the "goal pure and simple" on the basis of which the choice of factical possibilities becomes possible. This choice frees Dasein from contingent circumstances and brings it into "the simplicity of its fate." Indeed, Dasein, once freed from the illusions of the They by its appearing before death, is more radically attached to its factical situation than when it is "inauthentic" and irresolute. To say that "authentic" Dasein *is* fate (*Schicksal*) is but another way of saying that it is in a proper sense historical: the term *Schicksal*, like the term *Geschick*—the gathering of singular fates, or common fate—are derived, as is *Geschichte*, from the verb *geschehen*. Far from being borrowed, then, from the prevailing ideology of the time, this vocabulary is motivated by the way in which the German idiom conceives of history and historicality. But if *Schicksal* designates "authentic" historicality, which should be understood as "handing oneself down by anticipation to the 'there' of the moment of vision," this implies that history has its roots in the future rather than in the past: "*The finitude of temporality is the hidden basis of Dasein's historicality*" (BT, 438/386). For, if it is true that the explicit handing down takes place through a *repetition* of a possibility of existence that has been, one should not understand this repetition as a re-actualization of the past but rather as a *replica*, which, because it is the return of a *possible having been*, and not of something "past" [*dépassé*], is turned toward the future and thus discloses Dasein to its own history. Because fateful Dasein as Being-in-the-world is essentially Being-with-others, and because the possibilities it repeats come from others, its authentic destiny is guided from the common destiny which unites it with those with whom it shares the same world. This common destiny constitutes the full "authentic" historizing of Dasein.

Indeed, the historizing of history consists neither in the sequence of Experiences of subjects nor in the motions in the alterations of objects or in the way subject and object are linked together, but in the historizing of the world in its essential unity with Dasein, which Heidegger calls *world-history*. The historizing of intra-worldly entities is part of this world-history, the mobility of which cannot be understood as a merely local movement. It is because concernful Dasein is absorbed in the world that it first understands its history as a history of the world. The question of the "connectedness" of Dasein, existing in the dispersion of circumstances and opportunities, can only be posed in the horizon of everydayness, that is, on the basis of "inauthentic" historicality. Only an irresolute Dasein, in order to pull itself out of its dispersal, must *subsequently* think up for itself a unity. It is thus only for the "inauthentic" Dasein that the question of its unity is posed. Against the inconstancy of distraction, resoluteness, which alone constitutes the self, "is in itself *a steadiness which has been stretched along*—the steadiness with which Dasein as fate 'incorporates' into its existence, birth, and death, and their "between," and holds them as thus 'incorporated', so that in such constancy Dasein is indeed in a moment of vision for what is world-historical in its current situation" (BT, 442/390–391). Resoluteness, which is the loyalty of existence to itself, is not to be confused with the time that the act of resolving lasts. The steadiness that it gives to the self is not formed by the adjoining of moments one to another; rather, these arise from the temporality of anticipatory repetition, which has been already stretched along. "Authentic" temporality is thus a *de-presentation*. It is a de-actualization of the "today," the "inauthentic" present of the They. For, if inauthentic history seeks the modern in order to free itself from the weight of the past, "authentic" history, on the other hand, rests upon the "recurrence" of the possible. This explains why historiology, to the extent that it is based on Dasein's historicality, takes for its theme the possible, and not the actual, and why its point of departure is not the past but rather the future. "Authentic" historical science thus represents a science whose goal is not a making-present (a question left open in the note on page 414/363 of *Being and Time*) but instead temporalizes itself on the basis of the future. This, presumably, is the meaning of *destruction*, insofar as it constitutes a "specific mode of historical cognition" (BP, 23/32).

In 1936, in Rome, Heidegger told Karl Löwith that his concept of historicality was the basis for his 1933 engagement in National Socialism. It is indeed in the light of that particular chapter of *Being and Time* that Heidegger's political discourses as Rector should be read. In accepting the rectorship of the University of Freiburg, Heidegger pursued a goal that was nothing less than pedagogical: namely, that of a reform of knowledge, which, through the de-construction of a rigidified tradition, would root it again in its philosophical essence, a project that was diametrically opposed to the politicization of knowledge advocated by the Nazis, and also to the traditional ideal of a scientificity that would not understand theory as "the highest realization of genuine practice" (RA, 473). Heidegger found this pedagogical project in the work of Dilthey's friend and correspondent, Yorck von Wartenburg (who was actually the one who forged the term *Geschichlichkeit*), to which he devoted paragraph 77 of *Being and Time*, in which we find the following passage of a letter written by Yorck to Dilthey on 13 January 1883:

> But you are acquainted with my liking for paradox, which I justify by saying that paradoxicality is a mark of truth, and that the *communis opinio* is nowhere in the truth, but is like an elemental precipitate of a halfway understanding which makes generalizations; in its relation to truth it is like the sulphurous fumes which the lightning leaves behind. Truth is never an element. To dissolve elemental public opinion, and, as far as possible, to make possible the molding of individuality in seeing and looking, would be a pedagogical task for the state. Then, instead of a so-called public conscience—instead of this radical externalization—individual consciences—that is to say, consciences—would again become powerful.

3) WITHIN-TIME-NESS

Dasein is not simply temporal; as factical Dasein it is also "in time." The intratemporality of the time of concern also springs from Dasein's temporality and is therefore equiprimordial with historicality. It is thus necessary that the interpretation that factical Dasein gives of history, as happening within time, be *expressly* given its due. Indeed, the temporal analysis of Dasein will remain incomplete until it takes account of world-time (BT, 457/405). Now, in its Being-with others, Dasein remains in an average interpretation of time, which is articulated to the singular importance given to making-present. Heidegger calls the relational structure which unites a "now" with an "on that former occasion" and with a "then," *datability*. By means of datability, the making-present that is proper to concern interprets itself as being-alongside intra-worldly entities, in the sense that everyday ecstatic temporality also understands its horizon, the world of concern. This is why the datability of concern of a "now," a "then," and an "on that former occasion" *reflects* the ecstatical constitution of temporality as expressed in a presence alongside intra-worldy entities; the structures that stem from temporality are themselves "time." Yet, because Dasein forgets itself in concern, the discontinuous time that Dasein gives itself through the periodic articulation of the now in relation to the then remains hidden. This is why irresolute Dasein, insofar as it loses *itself* in the object of its concern, *loses its time*. On the other hand, "authentic" existence, which temporalizes itself by holding the present in the future that is in the process of having-been, as existence in the moment of vision, always has time for what the situation demands of it.

The time which is interpreted and expressed on the basis of Dasein's ecstatic Being-in-the-world is time made public. This publicness of time is based on the thrownness of Dasein, which must always *reckon with* time, although this reckoning should not be confused with the quantification of time. It is "in" this public time that intra-worldly entities are encountered, which explains why they are called *intratemporal*. Because Dasein, through its being-thrown, is delivered over to the changes of day and night, it dates the time of its concern in terms of the positions occupied by the sun; there arises the most natural measure of time, the day. Being-thrown, alongside entities ready-to-hand, is thus the basis for the natural clock that Dasein first uses. The natural clock makes possible the production and use of artificial clocks, which must be adjusted to it. This public time of concern is always a time that is either appropriate or inappropriate for some task; it thus manifests the structure of significance which constitutes the worldhood of the world. Regulating oneself according to the time by way of reading off the time on the clock can be explained as a *saying now*, which consists in the articulation of a distinctive making-present of an entity present-at-hand. It is indeed the function of measurement to make present an entity which can be present at any time ánd for everyone. The measurement of time thus makes time universally accessible as a present-at-hand multiplicity of nows. This "presence-at-hand" attributed to time does not, however, consist in a spatialization of time. What is indeed decisive in the measure of time is not that it takes place through our dating it in terms of spatial relations and in reference to the local motion of a spatial thing, but rather that it constitutes the specific *making-present* of an entity for everyone in every now in its own presence (BT, 471/418). Against the Bergsonian thesis of a qualitative duration that has been quantified and spatialized, Heidegger claims that intratemporality is a genuinely temporal (and not spatial) phenomenon, and that the ordinary concept of time based upon it should be accorded its due legitimacy (BT, 39/18 and 382/333). The time "within which" intra-worldly entities are encountered is nothing but world-time, which, like the world, is transcendent. Just as the world, world-time is neither simply subjective nor simply objective. It is (without, however, being identical to Kant's inner sense) the condition of the possibility of intra-worldly entities as well as the being of factical Dasein.

The time of concern, or world-time, becomes expressly accessible through the use of clocks. The counting of time becomes, through the use of clocks, the counting of the now in relation to the now that is no longer and the now that is not yet. Time is thus that which is numbered in movement encountered in the horizon of the earlier and later, which is precisely the Aristotelian definition of time in Book IV of *The Physics* (11 219b 1ff). The Aristotelian interpretation moves in the direction of the "natural" understanding of Being as *Vorhandenheit*, and does not question the origin of time that has thus been disclosed: it thematizes time as given in concern. The nows are that which is numbered as time. Heidegger calls the world-time that is "sighted" on the basis of the use of clocks the *now-time* (BT, 474/421). Time, indeed, shows itself, in ordinary understanding, as a pure succession, as a sequence of nows which are ontologically "sighted" in the horizon of the idea of presence-at-hand: they are co-present-at-hand with the entities, they pass away and come along: those which pass away constitute the past; those which come along constitute the future. Because the sequence of nows is itself conceived as "being in time," each now is *identified* with all the others: it is thus as constantly changing that the now manifests its constant presence, a phenomenon which lies at the basis of Plato's definition of time as the "image of eternity" (*Timaeus*, 37d). The thesis of a continuous and infinite time, which supposes that time is to be conceived as the "*free-floating 'in itself' of a course of 'nows' which is present-at-hand*" (BT, 476/424), is also based on this phenomenon. This infinitization of time rests on what Heidegger calls the "levelling-off" of world-time, which consists in the *covering up* of the structural items of the time of concern, which are datability, significance, and discontinuity. But this covering up is no accident: it necessarily occurs to the extent that, in everydayness,

Dasein only understands time in the horizon of concern without being able to grasp time as such, that is, by totally missing its source in ecstatical horizonal temporality. The finitude of temporality is thus covered up, although the fact of fleeing in the face of death, that is, the end of Being-in-the-world, is still a way of relating to death. Hence the idea of an infinity of a time in which the "they" never dies, if it is the case that death is each time mine and can only be understood in an existentiell manner in anticipatory resoluteness. Therefore the *ordinary* concept of time depends upon the They, which knows only the levelled-off public time that belongs to everyone, that is to say, is the temporality of nobody. However, the covering up of finite temporality is not total, as apparent from the fact that "ordinary" time is conceived as passing-away: only because Dasein is oriented toward the future can it understand the sequence of nows as an *irreversible succession*. The ordinary representation of time thus has its natural justification, since the conception of time as an endless, irreversible sequence of nows which passes away arises from the temporality of falling Dasein. This ordinary interpretation of time loses its justification only if it claims to convey the "true" conception of time, that is, if it ignores its derived *character*. For, while it may be possible to understand the ordinary representation of time on the basis of the primordial temporality of Dasein, the contrary is not possible: it is impossible to interpret the ecstatic, horizonal phenomenon of the moment of vision on the basis of the now (BT, 479/427).

However, isn't the fact that world-time is derived from Dasein's temporality the sign of a distinctive relation between time and the soul, or the mind—a relation that the philosophical tradition from Aristotle to Hegel, including St. Augustine and Kant, is far from having overlooked? In analyzing the Hegelian conception of the relation between time and spirit, Heidegger wants to show that his way of understanding the relation of Dasein to world-time is *opposed* to that of Hegel (BT, 457/405), whose concept of time represents "the most radical way in which the ordinary understanding of time has been given form conceptually" (BT, 480/428). Indeed, whereas Hegel, in order to explain the possibility of the historical realization of spirit as a "fall" of spirit "into" time, must suppose a kinship between spirit and time (each one conceived as being present-at-hand independently of each other), Heidegger, on the contrary, starts from the "concretization" of existence, that is, the relation that Dasein first entertains with the world, in order to reveal that which, as temporality, makes it possible. This is why, for Heidegger, "spirit" does not fall "into" time, for, on the contrary, it *exists* as the *temporalization* of temporality and as such provides the basis for both world-time and the intratemporality that are derived therefrom. There is, therefore, no fall of spirit *into* time, but a *falling* of factical existence *from* primordial temporality. Now, this existential difference between what is original and what is derived, between the authentic and the inauthentic, is not a "substantial" difference—as is the difference between spirit and time in

Hegel—but is rather an intrinsic difference in temporality itself, a difference between *two modes of temporalization*. The preliminary existential analysis and its repetition as temporal existential analysis have allowed us to account for the modal difference between inauthentic and authentic existence by leading them both back to their common basis: temporality.

3

◆

The Incompleteness of "Being and Time" and the Thinking of Ereignis

Der Abgrund ist die ursprüngliche Einheit *von Raum und Zeit, jene einigende Einheit, die sie erst in ihre Geschiednis auseinandergehen läßt.*

The abyss is the *primordial unity* of space and time, the uniting unity that lets them separate only in their divorce.

—*Beiträge zur Philosophie*, GA 65, 379

The last sentence of *Being and Time* is a question: "Is there a way which leads from primordial *time* to the meaning of *Being*? Does *time* itself manifest itself as the horizon of *Being*?" (BT, 488/437). Indeed, the existential-temporal analysis is only the *way* that one must follow in order to reach the *goal* that all philosophical research, as such, sets for itself, namely, not simply the analysis of the mode of Being of *one particular entity*, however "exemplary," but also the elaboration of the question of *Being as such*. Whether the way of the existential analytic is the *only* possible one, or even the right *one* at all, can only be decided, Heidegger explains, after one has gone along it (BT, 487/437). Yet, this way was interrupted before reaching its final stage. If, as the existential-temporal analysis has shown, the ontological constitution of Dasein as a whole is founded upon temporality, then it must also be a primordial mode of the temporalization of the temporality of Dasein that renders possible the ecstatical project of Being as such. The third division of the first part: "Time and Being," whose theme was to have been the "explication of time as the transcendental horizon for the question of Being," would have shown how what could be referred to as the "historicality" of Being itself is "founded" upon the temporality of Dasein. This, however, in no way means that Being would be "produced"

53

by man, for it is only as being-thrown that Dasein is able to project Being as such. This "projection of Being" is not caused by the *spontaneity* of a transcendental subject but, on the contrary, by the *facticity* of Dasein, which is not a subject precisely because it is not the cause [à l'*origine*]¹ of its own transcendence, but rather always already finds itself thrown into it. It is thus as Being-guilty that historical Dasein could understand its own Being as the "thrown basis" of the "history of Being." Yet, Heidegger did interrupt the publication of *Being and Time*, at the end of the second division, without covering this final stage, that is, without reaching the goal: *Being and Time* is an *incomplete* text. How are we to understand this incompleteness? Is it a sign that the way could not lead to the sought goal, and thus had to be abandoned in favor of another? Or, rather, did not the very following of the way lead Heidegger to understand his own thinking *in another way*, once the goal was attained?

It is Heidegger himself who in 1946, in *The Letter on Humanism* (BW, 208), spoke of "failure" (*Versagen* and *Scheitern*) with respect to the non-publication of the third division. Yet, this failure is not entirely negative, because the issue was not to abandon the attempt to think the relation between Being and time, as if that attempt had run into an impasse, but rather to think this relation otherwise than on the basis of Dasein's projection. Indeed, in running into the difficulty of what is in question for it, this thinking, far from distancing itself from it, *comes nearer* (BW, 208) to what it took as its task, namely, the historicality of Being. The fact that Heidegger, in 1927, chose not to publish his first version of the third division (we know that, judging it unsatisfactory, he burned it shortly after having written it) in no way implies that he abandoned from that moment the project of thinking the Temporality of Being in the light of the existential analytic. On the contrary, one can consider that all of his work up to 1930, in his courses and publications, was devoted to the elaboration of such a problematic and to the completion of *Being and Time*. Not only was his 1927 summer course, *The Basic Problems of Phenomenology*, presented as a "new elaboration of Division 3 of Part 1 of *Being and Time*" (BT, 1/1)—a note in the margin of Heidegger's personal copy of *Being and Time* confirms this, and refers the "Explication of Time as the Transcendental Horizon for the Question of Being" to that same course (BT, 65/41)—but the project of the second part of *Being and Time*, concerning the "basic features of a phenomenological destruction of the history of ontology, with the problematic of Temporality as our clue," was to a great extent also realized in the courses from 1925 through 1930: the Kantian doctrine of the schematism was analyzed in the 1925–26 course, *Logik* (GA 21), in the 1927–28 course, the *Phenomenological Interpretation of the "Critique of Pure Reason"* (GA 25), and in the 1929 book, *Kant and the Problem of Metaphysics*; the phenomenological destruction of Descartes's ontology and of his taking over of medieval ontology was the subject of paragraphs 10 through 12 of *The Basic Problems of*

Phenomenology (BT, 77–121/108–171) and of a 1923–24 course, *The Beginning of Modern Philosophy* (GA 17); as for the destruction of ancient ontology, focusing on Aristotle's treatise on time, one can find elements of it in courses from 1924–25, on *Plato's Sophist* (GA 19), and from the 1926 course, *The Fundamental Concepts of Ancient Philosophy* (GA 22), in *Logik* (GA 21), and in the 1930 course, *On the Essence of Human Freedom*. Heidegger thus did not abandon the problematic of the Temporality of Being. He simply did not want to put it in systematic form, presumably because this problematic had begun, as soon as the early thirties, to appear to him in a new perspective, no longer that (*transcendental-horizonal*) of a *meaning* of Being which would temporalize itself in the ecstatic temporality of Dasein, but rather that (*aletheiological-eksistential*) of a *truth* of Being *in* which Dasein stands and to which it has to correspond. The *turn*, or *turning* (*Kehre* or *Umkehr*: BW, 208), is that through which Being is taken as Temporal, no longer because it constitutes the horizonal unity of the ecstatical temporality of Dasein but, on the contrary, because, insofar as it is historical *in itself*, and not only through the intermediary of Dasein, it is Being itself which "sends man into the ek-sistence of Da-sein that is his essence" (BW, 217). Indeed, this reversal of the historicality of Dasein into a destiny or a history *of* Being (in the subjective sense of the genitive) already appears in the lecture "On the Essence of Truth," that Heidegger gave for the first time at Bremen in 1930, but was only published in 1943.

In that text, truth, which in *Being and Time* was a determination of Dasein itself—the Being of man is cleared in itself, Dasein being itself the *clearing* (BT, 171/133)—becomes a determination of Being itself, here thought of as the domain of the *open* (*das Offene*), as *aletheia*, from the Greek term for truth, which Heidegger now translates literally by *Unverborgenheit*, "unconcealment" (BW, 127–128). Existence, which in *Being and Time* designated the Being of Dasein as that entity which has a relationship to itself (BT, 32/12), is now written as *ek-sistence* and no longer designates Dasein's relation to itself but rather to the open, the "exposure to the disclosedness of beings as such" (BW, 128). It is on the basis of such a conception of the ek-sistence of man that he is said to have a historicality, which is a history of humanity only because it is primordially a *History of Being*: "That man ek-sists now means that for historical humanity the history of its essential possibilities is conserved in the disclosure or beings as a whole. The rare and the simple decisions of history arise from the way the original essence of truth essentially unfolds" (BW, 129–130). If Heidegger speaks of a "turning" in the self-interpretation of his path of thinking, it is because he considered that, in this transition from a history of Dasein to a history of Being, he did indeed reach his initial goal: "This turning is not a change of standpoint from *Being and Time*, but in it the thinking that was sought arrives at the location of that dimension out of which *Being and Time* is experienced, that is to say, experienced from the fundamental experience of the oblivion of Being" (BW, 208). Should one confirm Heidegger's self-interpretation and consider that this turning is not so much the parry of a thinker trapped in an impasse, or the turns taken by a meditative thought as a turning which takes place within the question itself, as he attempted to explain to Father Richardson (HPT, xviii)? This question can only be settled if one follows Heidegger up to the point where the "change of standpoint" corresponds to the turning of what is in question, that is, if, from the courses following *Being and Time* which are being published today in the complete edition, one follows to the end the development of the problematic envisioned at that time.

a) THE DEVELOPMENT OF TEMPORAL ONTOLOGY AS TRANSCENDENTAL SCIENCE FROM 1927 TO 1929

Temporality is the condition of possibility of the ontological constitution of Dasein and, therefore, must also be the condition of the understanding of Being that belongs to such a constitution. If time can be shown to be the horizon of the understanding of Being as such, ontology would then be established as a science, which is to say, the *thematization* of Being would find its guiding thread, on the basis of which a "genealogy of the different possible ways of Being (which is not to be constructed deductively)" (BT, 31/11) would be possible. In the introduction to *Being and Time*, Heidegger proposed to name the primordial determination of the meaning of Being (and of its modes) its *Temporal* determination (BT, 40/19). He clarified the meaning of this term in *The Basic Problems of Phenomenology*: while the German terms designating temporality are used in the context of the existential analytic, the Latin terms are used to indicate that the analysis operates at the level of the interpretation of Being on the basis of time (BP, 305/433). Now, the scientific elaboration of this interpretation requires that Being as such be *objectified*, thus uncovering the dimension that made possible the pre-scientific understanding of Being. The issue is thus to conceptualize Being, to question *beyond* Being itself toward that which makes the understanding of Being itself possible, and not simply that of beings. The elaboration of the Temporality of Being thus consists in the attempt to conceive what Plato designated in the allegory of the sun, in *The Republic*, as the *epekeina tēs ousias*, as the beyond of Being which "has the function of light, of illumination, for all unveiling of beings or, in this case, illumination for the understanding of being itself" (BP, 284/402). But, because there is Being only through Dasein's understanding, bringing out the Temporality of Being cannot consist in elaborating an all-encompassing concept of time—the unity of the meaning of Being is not generic (BT, 22/3) —but rather in the explication of the Temporality of Being *on the basis of* Dasein's temporality. It is thus the latter that makes ontology as a science possible and is therefore called Temporality: "The term 'Temporality'

[*Temporalität*] . . . means temporality [*Zeitlichkeit*] insofar as temporality itself is made into a theme as the condition of the possibility of the understanding of being and of ontology as such" (BP, 228/324). This is why we translate the German and Latin terms by one single word, while only differentiating them by an upper-case letter: there are not two different phenomena, but *one*, seen from two different perspectives.

It is thus a question of showing how Temporality makes the understanding of Being possible. If that understanding is itself made possible by the fundamental constitution of Dasein as Being-in-the-world, we are then referred to the Temporal problem of the transcendence of the world, which *Being and Time* treated laconically in paragraph 69c. With respect to the question of the meaning of Being, this short paragraph represents the culminating point of the text: it affirms the unity of the Being of *Dasein* and of the world by showing how the world is also founded in temporality. In a long footnote in *The Essence of Reasons*, a text dedicated to Husserl for his seventieth birthday, whose central theme is *transcendence*, Heidegger nonetheless argues forcefully that "giving an ontological interpretation of Being in and from the transcendence of Dasein does not amount to undertaking an ontical deduction which is not of the order of *Dasein*, from that entity which *Dasein* is, precisely because if *Dasein* comes thus to the 'center' of the ontological problematic, it is as 'ecstatic or excentric' (ER, 99). The Heideggerian concept of transcendence is indeed directed against the representation of the interiority of the subject as a "box" or "cabinet" (BT, 87/60), on the basis of which the false problem of the relation of the immanence of consciousness to what is transcendent to it arises (BP, 214/306). Because Heidegger wants to show that, as Being-in-the-world, Dasein has nothing in common with the subject in the modern sense of the term, he rejects the traditional opposition between immanence and transcendence that, despite the plurality of meanings that Husserl gave to these concepts, still governs the problematic of an intentionality of consciousness. For Heidegger, things are not transcendent; rather, it is what the tradition has conceived of as an immanent subject which is the authentic transcendent, for *epekeina* belongs to the most proper ontological structure of Dasein. Dasein is not a subject that would then transcend toward objects; rather, it is Selfhood itself which is possible only on the basis of transcendence. Dasein transcends beings as a whole *toward* the world, which is transcendent because it belongs to the structure of Being-in-the-world, and not because it would be constituted by the sum of "transcendent" objects in the traditional sense (BP, 300/425). On the basis of this sense of transcendence it is possible to understand intentionality, not only on the basis of the *intentio* of the "subject" and the *intentum* of the "object," but also on the basis of the "understanding of the mode of being of what is intended in the "*intentum*," which constitutes the ontological condition of its possibility. Indeed, intentional comportment only uncovers beings, which presupposes the prior disclosedness of the Being of the being (BP, 71/100–101). If every relation to beings presupposes the understanding of their Being, it implies that intentionality, far from making transcendence possible, is possible only on the basis of it (ER, 29).

The problematic of transcendence thus allows one to reveal the beyond of Being which constitutes the horizon of its comprehensibility, without leaving the "sphere" of Dasein, since Dasein is precisely defined as *epekeina*. The ecstatic character of time is thus the basis for Dasein's transcendence, for it is what makes the overstepping toward the world possible, to the extent that the ecstases of temporality each have a horizon proper to them. The structural unity of transcendence and world must be understood, then, as the unity of the ecstases of temporality and their horizonal schemata. If transcendence is that which makes the understanding of Being possible, and if the basis for transcendence is the original ecstatic-horizonal unity of temporality, the latter is then the condition for the understanding of Being (BP, 302/429). Being is, indeed, understood on the basis of the horizonal schemata of temporality. Their unity (the world) represents that beyond of Being which constitutes the horizon from which Being is always already understood pre-ontologically. It is thus clear that it was by considering the whole of temporality, that is, the inseparable unity of ecstases and horizons, that Heidegger formed the concept of *Temporality* (*Temporalität*): "The temporality which is thus primarily carried away to the horizonal schemata of temporality [*Zeitlichkeit*] as conditions of the possibility of the understanding of being, constitutes the content of the general concept of Temporality [*Temporalität*]. *Temporality* [*Temporalität*] is *temporality* [*Zeitlichkeit*] with regard to the unity of the horizonal schemata belonging to it*" (BP, 307/436). Heidegger thus uses the concept of *Temporalität* in both a narrow and broad sense. In the broad sense, it designates *Zeitlichkeit* as the condition of the possibility for the understanding of Being (BP, 274/389); in the narrow sense, it simply designates the horizonal schema of *Zeitlichkeit* (BP, 312/444). In these two cases, however, it is the concept of "horizonal schema" that must be defined in order to understand what Heidegger means when he defines ontology as a Temporal science.

Heidegger is most explicit on the concept of horizon. In his 1928 course, which bears in part on the Leibnizian theory of judgment, Heidegger explains that the term "horizon," from the Greek *horizein*, is not primarily related to looking and intuition but simply means: that which delimits and encloses (MFL, 208/269). He thus moves away from the modern concept of horizon, which from Leibniz to Husserl designates both the infinite realm of the knowable and the limits of clear possible knowledge. Indeed, the issue for Heidegger is no longer to relate "horizonality" to knowledge, but rather to its origin, Care. An horizon does not constitute the field of theoretical vision, but rather the domain of projection. As a structural moment of temporality, an horizon must be understood as that which constitutes the *enclosure* of the ecstatic opening. Certainly, ecstasis itself must be seen as a movement of overstepping, that is to say, as the boundlessness of transcendence and the opening to the indefinite. Nevertheless, at the same time, it is not *in itself* an indefinite opening, though it does produce the dimension of the future, that is, of possibility as such. It is thus the horizonal structure of temporality that makes possible the opening of Dasein to Being and to beings. As condition for the opening to the *other*, horizon cannot itself be thematized; it cannot therefore constitute a correlate of ecstasis, even though it is inseparable from it. If, in the 1928 course, Heidegger calls *ekstêma* the horizon that appears in and with *ekstasis*, it is, however, in a sense fundamentally different from the unity of *noêsis* and *noêma*, which in Husserl's work is "immanent" to consciousness. The horizon, contrary to the *noema*, which is immanent (although, to be sure, not in a real, but intentional sense), is not located in the sphere of the subject. It is, moreover, neither spatially nor temporally located, for it "is" not at such; rather, it temporalizes itself (MFL, 208/269). This explains why horizon evades not only the modern way of thinking, according to which all beings are constituted in consciousness, but also the existential-ontological way of thinking, which could only explain the horizon by showing that which makes it possible, with the result of destroying the very structure of the horizon as such. Because the horizon represents the condition of possibility for a general movement of overstepping, it is not possible to question what in turn makes possible the horizonal schema: in the horizon, temporality meets its *end*,[2] which is nothing other than the beginning and the starting-point of the possibility of all projecting (BP, 308/437). If horizons cannot be understood but from themselves, this implies that it is not possible to completely objectify and analyze the conditions of possibility of temporality by separating them, as it were, from what they make possible, namely, the concrete factical existence of Dasein (BP, 327/465). This is the meaning of the claim found in paragraph 65 of *Being and Time*: "Primordial time is finite" (BT, 379/331). This finitude must be understood, not in an external way, in opposition to the infinite sequence of nows succeeding each other on the timeline, but as that structural finitude of primordial time which alone makes possible the representation of the infinite time of the now. This implies that the *enclosure* of the horizon should be understood in a positive rather than negative manner: insofar as it constitutes the *end* of the ecstatical movement, the horizon is at the same time the *beginning* of the uncovering of beings. No more than death does the horizon constitute an external limit for Dasein. In *Being and Time*, death "*as the end of Dasein*" is, in fact, defined as "*Dasein's ownmost possibility—non-relational, certain and as such indefinite, not to be outstripped*" (BT, 303/258). All these determinations could apply as well to the horizonal structure of temporality, in particular the unsupersedable character which indicates that the horizon constitutes the a priori limit inherent to all projection while at the same time opening its possibility. The horizonality of Temporality expresses, then, the positive character of finitude, in the sense that the positive becomes essentially clear when seen from the side of the negative (BP, 309/439). It is indeed Dasein's dependency on a pre-given being that requires the production of a horizon within which the being which is present-at-hand is able to appear. It is precisely because the human *intuitus* is *ontically* non-creative that it must be *ontologically* creative, in what Kant calls the *exhibitio originaria* of the productive synthesis of imagination (GA 25, 417).[3] We must here clarify the notion of "schema," in reference to Heidegger's interpretation of the Kantian schematism as the "advent of transcendence" (KPM, 69). In Kant, the concept of schema designates not an empirical image but the representation of the rule on the basis of which anything can be represented. Pure imagination, by forming the schema, provides, in advance, a "look" for whatever could present itself. The transcendental schema, for Heidegger, is then the prefiguration of what will be able to present itself as a being. Thus, what Kant discovered in his theory of schematism is "the primordial productivity of the subject," which Heidegger understands as the intrinsic, primordial productivity of Temporality (MFL, 210–211/272). Indeed, *self-projection* (*Selbstentwurf*) (BP, 309/439) is what characterizes Temporality. By seeking to make of Kant "an advocate for the question of Being," Heidegger was led to "overinterpret" (such are his own terms in the Preface to the fourth edition of the *Kantbuch*: cf. KPM, xv and xvi) the Kantian theory of self-affection in the sense of a pure self-affection of time (KPM, paragraph 34). For Heidegger, the affection of inner sense can only have the sense of a self-activating (*Sich-selbstangehen*) by which the structure of subjectivity forms itself. Only on the basis of this selfhood can the finite being be dependent on receptivity, in the sense that pure affection consists in providing an op-position for this being. It is clear that self-affection allows us to conceive of the co-belonging of the structural moments of transcendence—ecstasis and horizon—without, however, ascribing it to an act of the subject, but rather to the temporalization of Temporality. The ecstases thus predelineate for themselves the look from which they can operate as specific modes of disclosure. They are therefore the basis for what makes them comprehensible, namely, the horizonal schemas. This is why Heidegger, in the *Essence of Reasons*, determined freedom as "the ground of ground." However, because freedom is finite, that is to say, because it is not its own ground, it is precisely, as ground (*Grund*), the abyss (*Abgrund*) of Dasein (ER, 127 and 129, trans. modified).

In *The Basic Problems of Phenomenology*, the only example of Temporal interpretation that Heidegger gives is that of Being in the sense of pure presence-at-hand (*Vorhandenheit*), because he had set out to take account of the positive content of the Kantian thesis about Being—Being is not a real predicate—which he formulates in the following way: Being present-at-hand is absolute position or perception (BP, 313/445). Perception, as intentional comportment, is a distinctive mode of presentation. The ecstasis of the present is therefore the fundamental basis for the specifically intentional transcendence of the perception of the being present-at-hand. To ecstasis as such belongs a horizonal schema, which, in the case of the present, is the *praesens* (the recourse to the Latin term indicating here that it is a question of a horizonal, as opposed to an ecstatic, phenomenon). Presentation, as an ecstatic movement, projects what it presents toward *praesentia* (BP, 306/435). The Temporal meaning of Being as presence-at-hand is *presence (Anwesenheit, Praesenz)*. It thus appears that Kant implicitly understood Being in the same manner as ancient philosophy did: the entire tradition understands Being on the basis of the present, taking its lead from Dasein's everyday understanding of beings (BP, 315/448). The Kantian proposition—that (present-at-hand) Being is position—can be fully understood only in its Temporal interpretation; "existence," as a logical (not real) predicate, cannot be derived from beings themselves, but must on the contrary be already disclosed in the self-projection of the present as horizonal schema of *praesentia*, for beings to be able to be encountered as "existent" (BP, 317/451).

The Temporal analysis of Being in the sense of presence-at-hand has shown that it is the horizonal schema of *praesentia* that prescribes, both to the intentional comportment of Dasein and to the uncovering of entities, their specific modalities. One understands why the ecstases do not by themselves constitute the basis of Being-in-the-world; without the horizonal schemata from which Dasein intentionally *comes back* to beings, intentionality itself would be incomprehensible. There is therefore no comportment toward beings that does not understand Being, and there is no understanding of Being that is not based on a comportment toward beings (BP, 327/466). Being is, indeed, the horizonal opening produced by the self-projection of the ecstasis from which the intentional comportment made possible by the ecstasis understands itself, so that a definite uncovering of beings can occur. What then defines the existence of Dasein, insofar as this existence is based on temporality, is "the immediate unity of the understanding of Being and comportment toward beings" (BP, 319/454). It is, indeed, the structure of temporality that constitutes the entity that Dasein is—an entity which is always already "outside," alongside the entities which it is not, and which at the same time has a relation to itself. Because the distinction between Being and beings belongs to Dasein's existence, it is already there in a latent manner, even if it is not expressly known. For, if existence means, as it were, "to be in the performance of this distinction," it implies that this distinction "*is temporalized in the temporalizing of Temporality*" (BP, 319/454), which means that it is not merely present-at-hand but is, rather, that ability to differentiate (ER, 27, trans. modified) which occurs on the basis of and with Temporality. Now, this capacity-to-differentiate should be understood as a capacity-to-schematize: it becomes clear, then, that it has to do with what Heidegger calls, in *Being and Time*, "the schema of the as-structure," through which the understanding of Being pre-predicatively becomes explicit to itself and which is predicatively expressed in the "is" of the copula (BT, 411/360). The existential analysis of schematization could thus take account of the fact that the discourse in which it is articulated cannot refer to the opening of a particular ecstasis but rather to the horizonal unity of the schemata, that is, to the world itself. In the 1929–30 winter semester course devoted particularly to the question of the world, *The Fundamental Concepts of Metaphysics*, Heidegger, through the thesis that man, in contrast with animals that are "poor in world," is "world-*forming*" (*welt* bilden), related this capacity for schematization or prefiguration, which Kant attributed to imagination (*Ein*bildungs*kraft*), to the phenomenon of language (GA 29–30, 483ff). It is thus because the distinction between Being and beings is always already in some way disclosed in any human comportment that it can be expressly known and conceptually apprehended. When it is explicitly understood, Heidegger names this distinction the *ontological difference* (BP, 319/454). Ontology is based on a fundamental comportment of Dasein, because its possibility, that is, the possibility of philosophy as science, depends on the possibility of performing the distinction between Being and beings in a sufficiently clear manner (BP, 227/322).

Because transcendence makes the objectification of Being possible, the science of Being is a *transcendental science*, in a sense more primordial than Kant's. Because, as was shown, the horizon of the comprehensibility of Being, that is to say, its transcendental horizon, is time, the science of Being is a *Temporal science*; consequently, all its propositions have the character of the *veritas temporalis* (BP, 323/460). This implies giving up the traditional idea of the absolute and eternal nature of truth. Indeed, it appears that the ideal of objectivity is linked to only *one* meaning of Being, namely, presence-at-hand, which not only is not the only meaning of Being possible, but moreover presupposes Dasein's transcendence. The ontology of *Vorhandenheit*, that is, traditional ontology as a whole, constitutes no more than a *region* of Temporal ontology, which extends further than the sole domain of objective knowledge (GA 25, 200). One understands better, on this basis, the meaning of the debate between Heidegger and Cassirer at Davos in 1929. Cassirer, who wished to maintain the Kantian ideal of objectivity, accused Heidegger of relativism (KPM, 173). Heidegger responded by showing that the very idea of eternal truth presupposes the transcendence of Dasein, that is, the intrinsic possibility for this finite being to produce the horizon of permanence and presence. This implies that there is no philosophy which can be free from a point of view, for, if philosophy's task is not that of providing a world-view, the very act of philosophizing nevertheless presupposes a world-view (KPM, 178). The historicality of truth is thereby affirmed, which in no way leads to a relativism and a historicism, but on the contrary allows the destruction of traditional ontology, that is, reveals the concealed existential origin of the ontological concepts of universal scope. Temporal ontology is thus not a "theory" in the traditional sense, even if Heidegger characterizes it as a "science" of Being, for the objectification of Being it requires does not have the sense of a *presentation*, as is the case in the ontical sciences, but rather of an explication of transcendence (KPM, 165). This prevents ontology from being completely detached from its concrete existential roots. Because it is only possible in connection with its ontical foundation (BT, 487/436), Temporal ontology avoids the twofold threat that had constantly threatened ontology up to this point: the dissolution of the whole of the ontical in the ontological, as in the case of Hegelianism, or the pure and simple evacuation of the ontological in ontical explications, as in the case of positivism (BP, 327/466). Temporal ontology, indeed, claims to be "universal phenomenological ontology, and takes its departure from the hermeneutic of Dasein, which, as an analytic of *existence*, has made fast the guiding-line for all philosophical inquiry at the point where it *arises* and to which it *returns*" (BT, 62/38; 487/436).

b) THE TURN OF EREIGNIS AND THE 1962 LECTURE

To the extent that philosophizing no longer consists in taking refuge in pure theory but, on the contrary, in exposing itself to what Heidegger calls, in a 1931 course, the *offensive* character of the question of Being—which, far from being a general question, directly reaches the very roots of the singular being (GA 31, 131)—Heidegger's political engagement in 1933 can only be understood on the basis of his philosophical engagement. Indeed, only by relating them both to the idea of a finitude of Being itself (and not only of Dasein), and to the conception of an intrinsically Temporal meaning of truth, can one understand how Heidegger, in his *Rectoral Address*, could have characterized the essence of science as the "completely unguarded exposure to the hidden and uncertain, i.e., the questionable," which characterizes "the forsakeness of modern man in the midst of what is" after the death of God (RA, 474). The intention of leading scattered disciplines back to their common philosophical essence, that is, the fact of exposing "science once again to the fertility and the blessing bestowed by all the world-shaping powers of human-historical being (*Dasein*)," (RA, 474) refers to the project of a fundamental ontology, or a "metaphysics of Dasein" that would be effected as a Temporal ontology. At the same time, however, one can already see in the *Rectoral Address*, by way of a citation from Aeschylus, who speaks of the weakness of knowledge before necessity, the emergence of the notion of destiny that would be one of Being itself, and not only of Dasein, and which would unfold as the power of a constant concealment of beings as a whole (RA, 472). It is, indeed, during the years following the Rectorate episode—and as a philosophical response to his "mistake" of 1933–34—that Heidegger elaborated, with the term *Ereignis*, a new conception of Being, considered no longer as the ground of beings (this is why from this period on he would prefer to use the ancient spelling *Seyn*) but as the unfolding of the clearing from an *abyssal* withdrawal and concealment. Because man is no longer the thrown basis of this clearing but rather stands *in* it and is *indebted* to it for his own Being, Dasein will then be written as Da-sein, in order to indicate by this new rendering that the "there" of Being can no longer be understood as the Being that Dasein projects through *self*-projection and as *self*-affection, but as the call (*Anspruch*) *of* Being itself *to* man, a call to which man corresponds (*entspricht*) through thought. It is this *non-coincidence* of the Being of man and of Being as such which explains that the forgetting of Being is not so much the fault of metaphysical thinking as what constitutes the very *"ownness"* of Being, which withdraws, that is to say, forgets itself by *making* the clearing *possible*. This is why Heidegger henceforth understands by Da-sein the relation of Being to man. The term *Verhältnis*, which then appears (BW, 211) and usually means relation, must essentially be understood from the holding back (*Verhaltenheit*) that constitutes the fundamental mood of a thinking, which corresponds to the reserve (*Vor-enthalt*) and to the withdrawal of Being itself.

It is this co-*belonging*, which is neither coincidence nor coordination, but rather the reciprocal relation and constellation of man and Being, that Heidegger calls *Ereignis* (cf. *Identity and Difference*), a term which became the guiding term of his thought as early as the mid-thirties. For example, a manuscript of more than five hundred pages written by Heidegger during 1936–38, *Contributions to Philosophy* (*On "Ereignis"*), was recently published. Its publisher presents this text as Heidegger's second major work after *Being and Time*. It is there, in fact, that the turn is experienced, of which Heidegger has said that he neither invented it nor that it concerned his thought alone (HPT, xviii), and which he understood as the "turn of *Ereignis*" or "turn in *Ereignis*" (GA 65, 407 and 409). Heidegger does not consider *Ereignis*, which names the relation of what is in question in "Being *and* time" and in "time *and* Being" (TB, 4), to be a terminological decision peculiar to him but, instead, the highest gift of the German idiom, comparable to the Greek *aletheia* (HPT, xxii) or, as well, to the Chinese *Tao* (ID, 36). According to him, language is not left to arbitrary human invention but is itself the most proper mode of *Ereignis*; it is its melody that deploys itself through our corresponding and thanking saying (OWL, 135). This is why *Ereignis*, which in modern German means "event," must be understood on the basis of its etymological sense, which pertains first not to *eignen* and to *eigen*, to propriety and appropriation, but to *Auge*, to the eye and to seeing: it means to eye. *Ereignen* as *eräugen* thus signifies bringing to ownness by making visible. *Ereignis*, by making visible the unfolding of the Being of man as Da-sein in the clearing, brings the mortals to their own by making them appropriate (*vereignen*) to Being, which, for its part, is appropriated (*zugeeignet*), that is to say, given over to the Being of man (OWL, 128–129). What Heidegger understands by this term is the reciprocal owning of Being and man, through which they are related. But because *Ereignis* is then the relation of all relations (OWL, 135), what is most proper to it is its expropriation—*Enteignis* (TB, 23)—just as concealment, or *lethe*, belongs to the visibility of *aletheia*, which occurs as *Lichtung*, or clearing, as that which is most proper to it, as its heart (TB, 71). It is precisely because *Ereignis* does not have the structure of selfhood, because it can only be thought as a sending (*Schicken*), that is to say, a giving which gives only its very givenness and as such holds itself back and withdraws (TB, 8), that it is in itself *Enteignis*, that is, the groundless ground of Being, its abyss. It is only at this point that Heidegger truly breaks with the idea of the absolute that governed the entire history of thought. For, the finitude of Being, which is still discussed in the texts from 1929 (for example in "What Is Metaphysics?" BW, 110) is still thought in relation to the transcendence of Dasein, whose being is a finite horizon, that is, in relation to the in-finitude of a self-projection which closes on itself, while the finitude of *Ereignis* comes from the intrinsic limit of destiny, which, as sending, must be secure in one's own abyssal withdrawal (TB, 54). The finitude of *Ereignis* is thought of on the basis of the concept of propriety, which Heidegger wants to distinguish from the concept of selfhood: propriety is that which belongs to something, what allows it to be what it is, and not what makes it a "subject" capable of taking possession of an *other* thing. In this sense, the Heideggerian concept of *Eigentum* has nothing in common with a possession that is understood as privatization, as the Latin *proprius* (from *pro-privus*) indicates.[4] This new concept of finitude requires the abandonment of transcendental thinking and "the overcoming of the horizon as such," as Heidegger noted in the margin of his personal copy of *Being and Time*.[5] The concept of horizon, in fact, proves insufficient to give thought to the domain of opening, the open within which beings can be encountered, for it is "but the side facing us of an openness which surrounds us" (DT, 64), an openness that should be called *Gegnet*, or "region" in the sense of a "free expanse" (*freie Weite*) (DT, 66). It is thus, indeed, a question of leaving the enclosure of the horizon in order to think the proper gap that belongs to the far—the German *Weite* has the same root as the Latin *vitium*, of which the primary meaning is "gap"— which forbids reducing the spatiality of Dasein to temporality, as Heidegger attempted in paragraph 70 of *Being and Time* (TB, 23). To give thought to what is proper to space, that is to say, *spacing* as the releasing of a free space, the opening of a clearing (Q IV, 101), is in fact only possible from the perspective of *Ereignis* understood as destiny—*Geschick*. For, *schicken* originally meant to organize in the sense of making room, *einräumen*: this is why, when Heidegger uses the word *Geschick* about Being, he means "nothing other than the proffering of the lighting and clearing that furnishes a domain for the appearing of beings" (PR, 88). *Lichtung*, "the clearing," must be itself thought on the basis of *Geschick*. Whereas in *Being and Time* as well as in later texts (even in the lecture *The Turning*, delivered in 1949 but published in 1962, cf. QCT, 47), this term is related to light (*Licht*) and illumination, in *The End of Philosophy and the Task of Thinking* (1964), it is instead related to a completely different sense of the verb *Lichten*, which does not mean "to illuminate" but rather "to make a free space," "making light in the sense of bringing about a clearing" (TB, 65). Light and the realm of visibility as a whole are thus subordinated to the open of the *Lichtung* as clearing, to the making room of that field of play where presence and absence, light and darkness, appropriation and expropriation testify to their co-belonging.

One can understand, on the basis of the full extent of the "turning of *Ereignis*," that when Heidegger gave the 31 January 1962 lecture *Time and Being*, that text could no longer be understood in relation to the 1927 text *Being and Time*. If what is at issue is the same question—that of the *and*, in Being *and* Time and in Time *and* Being, it can no longer be posed on the basis of a transcendence which stills draws from Platonism, but rather from the *movement of givenness* that Platonic metaphysics did not think but constantly presupposed. Because Being is neither extant nor simply temporal, and because time is neither temporal nor simply extant, one is able to say of them not that they *are* but that *there is* Being and that *there is* time—in German, *es gibt*, "it gives." This impersonal phrase appeared in *Being and Time* (for example, BT, 255/212), but to indicate the ontological difference, that is to say, that which makes the "is" of beings possible. In this new context, it is no longer a question of a transcendental potentiality-to-differentiate of Dasein but of the twofoldness (*Zwiefalt*) of Being itself which conceals itself in favor of the unconcealment of beings (EP, 90). What must be thought, then, if time and Being are given, is what is given each time as well as that which gives. Now, Being means presence—*Anwesen*. In German, this term literally means "proceeding into Being": that which is "present," *anwesend*, is what is brought forth in un-concealment. Being, insofar as it brings forth beings in non-concealment, is thus a letting-be set forth in presence. Yet, this unconcealment of beings is itself made possible by a second "letting," which is the gift of the unfolding of presence, that is, of Being itself (TB, 5 and 37). Being, when no longer thought of as the ground of beings, that is, when thought of in what is proper to it, is the gift of the unfolding of presence. This gift remains unthought in the *esti gar enai*, "there is indeed Being," of Parmenides. But this unthought does not achieve conceptual clarity in Heidegger's thought, since this givenness is a *sending*, that is, a gift without a "subject" who gives. As a destiny, Being is historical in itself; but the history of Being is not accomplished with the thought of *Ereignis*, that is, the thought of that which gives and sends, as it is accomplished in

Hegel's work—in an absolute knowledge, through the identification of Being and thinking—for that which gives the unfolding of presence cannot itself enter into presence (TB, 50). The epochs of the history of Being are not, as they are in Hegel's work, periods of time but, on the contrary, the fundamental characteristic of the sending which *withholds itself*—this is the proper meaning of the Greek *epoche*—for it to be givenness. It is this epochal essence of the destining that permits the historicality of the thought which responds to it to be understood (TB, 9–10). Since 1946, in the *Anaximander Fragment*, the ecstatic character of Dasein was presented as *corresponding* to the epochal character of the history of Being, and no longer as the basis of that history. Indeed, epochality characterizes "the essence of time as thought in Being" (EGT, 27), that is, that becoming without a subject that Heidegger names destining, of which we find the first mention in Hölderlin's essay to which Heidegger alludes briefly in his course in the summer of 1941–42 (GA 52, 119). It is only on the basis of what Nietzsche called the "innocence" of becoming, that is to say, on the basis of a conception which no longer sees the temporal realization of the atemporal in history, that true eternity can be thought: it is not at all the permanence of a subsisting being but, on the contrary, the enigmatic constancy of the withdrawal itself, which appears in the suddenness of the instant, in the sudden flash of the coming into presence (PR, 95).

What becomes of the giving of time itself? When we determine what is proper to time on the basis of the *present* (*Gegenwart*), we generally understand it in terms of the now, as opposed to the coming into presence (*Anwesenheit*). Yet, the present, understood from the coming into presence, has the sense of a coming *toward* us in order to dwell there (*entgegenweilen*), for, in the *gegen* of *Gegenwart*, one hears the relation of presence to man: man is thus the one to whom the coming to presence is addressed. In presence understood as *Anwesen*, man's relation to Being is revealed: man is only man because Being itself addresses itself to him in the unfolding of presence, and not because he is, in virtue of his ecstatic essence, the "place" of the self-address of Being (TB, 12). The *future* will then no longer be thought of as the coming *to itself* of Dasein, but as the coming *of* Being *to* man. This is why Heidegger, in a 1958 text, *The Principles of Thinking*, could say that, rightly thought, the future is an attending present (*Gegen-wart*), for with this term he understands not what happens to be here now, for the moment, but rather what waits (*wartet*) for our encounter (*entgegen*), whether and how we expose ourselves to it (PT, 48, and OWL, 106). What Heidegger called in 1946 the eschatological character of Being (EGT, 18) in no way refers to the dimension of the future, but only to the present understood in this sense, that is, to the *necessity* of what comes toward us, to which we respond by letting come toward us that which is not simply the "past" but the having-been. Only then can we anticipate "the former dawn in the dawn to come" (EGT, 18). This unfolding of presence, which constantly concerns man, is not thus necessarily in the present in the sense of being opposed to the future and to the having been: any *Anwesen* is not *Gegenwart*, since the absence of the having-been as well as that of the future remains a mode of the coming into presence which addresses itself to us. That which is proper to time, then, is constituted by the fact that it is in itself this *givenness from a distance* that is expressed by the German *reichen* which literally means to extend, to present in the sense of to give in a movement of extension ahead, and which refers to the idea of an extended power, of a *realm*, or of a directionality of time (*reichen* has the same root as Latin *reg-*, which gave *rex* and *dirigere*). Time is thus itself the unity of this threefold givenness, from a distance of the having-been through the future and the future through the having-been, which in their reciprocal relation produce the present (TB, 13–14). Heidegger calls space-time (*Zeitraum*) the clearing that is open through the reciprocal givenness, from a distance, of the future of the having-been and the present. *Dimensionality* pertains to time but should be understood not in a simply spatial sense as a domain of possible measuring but as the very givenness of measure. But, if a specific modality of coming into presence is in play in each of the three dimensions of time, it is not possible to refer it to the present alone: the reciprocal *play* of each of the dimensions of time—through which each gives the others and is given through them—constitutes a fourth dimension of time, which is in fact the first since the givenness from a distance of presence resides therein. Heidegger proposes to understand it as *nearness*, in the sense that it allows the neighboring of the dimensions of time by preventing and withholding their fusion. The opening of the clearing is thus ensured in advance by the holding in reserve of that which is prevented in the having-been and of that which is withheld in the future (TB, 15–16). This realm of time reaches man, who is only man because he stands in its threefold dimensionality and is exposed to this givenness, which is at the same time withheld.

The destinal givenness of Being and the extensive givenness of time, in the epochal withholding for one and in the preventing and the reserve of the present in the future and the having-been for the other, manifest the same withdrawal through which *Ereignis* guards that which is proper to it and preserves it from an unlimited un-concealment, which would moreover amount to an unlimited concealment. It is on the basis of *Ereignis* that Being and time are determined in what is proper to them, that is, in their co-belonging. But, no more than Being, in what is proper to it, is the ground of beings can time be said to be, in what is proper to it, the ground of Being, although the destining that gives Being rests upon the realm of time (TB, 17). This is why, as Heidegger indicates in the beginning of *The End of Philosophy and the Task of Thinking*, the resumption of the attempt to "shape the question of Being and Time in a more primal way," which has been "undertaken again and again ever since 1930" (TB, 55), could well lead to changing the title of the task undertaken with *Being and Time* (TB, 55). Because Being thought on the basis of the clearing is destinal presence, and because the clearing thought on the basis of *Ereignis* is time itself, the task of thinking would thus be called, in the place of Being and time, *Lichtung und Anwesenheit*, clearing and presence (TB, 73). With this title, which names the unthought of philosophy, the proper matter of thought—*die Sache selbst, to pragma auto*—is determined. In fact, philosophy, since Plato, has always been concerned with such a question. This is why the abandonment of thought in its philosophical mode in no way led Heidegger to the overcoming of metaphysics but rather to its appropriation.

4

◆

Remarks on the Translation of Key Terms[1]

To pay heed to what the words say is different in essence from what it first seems to be, a mere preoccupation with terms.

—WCT, 130

Heidegger's thought, probably more than any other, is inseparable from the idiom in which it is expressed. One should add that Heidegger represents only the extreme case of what is normal for any thought, namely, attempting to express a universal in and through a singular language. We know, at least since Herder and especially since Humboldt (under whose authority Heidegger explicitly places himself [OWL, 116; 136]), that every language is a world-view and is, therefore, not a mere *tool* for expressing preexisting significations but instead *constitutes* them. This is why translating can never be a simple transposition of terms from one language to another or the search for interlinguistic equivalences. The translation of a signification of one language into another necessarily demands the interpretative appropriation of the *foreign signification.* That translation is nevertheless possible is what Heidegger himself stresses when he recalls, in a course from the winter semester 1942–43 (GA 54, 17), that we must first translate our own mother tongue, that is, appropriate this idiom, which is never only a familiar tool but, as soon as we begin to think, acquires the status of a foreign language. It is this translation within language that makes the translation between different languages possible. This, however, implies that translating is always a work of *thought* and an effort of *interpretation.*

This conception of translation led me to translate anew the entirety of the passages cited in what precedes. This in no way should be taken as a sign of contempt for extant translations, on which I have constantly relied. I happen to view the fact that there are several translations (partial and complete) of *Being and Time* as an advantage rather than as a problem: I drew inspiration from each of them, for they each have their strengths and their weaknesses

71

(and even their weaknesses have their virtues).[2] I do not believe that any translation can be considered complete and definitive, nor that it can represent a self-sufficient equivalent of the original text it translates. A translation does not *replace* the original text but only *refers* to it; it thus can only attempt to give access to it as well as possible. This is exactly what my interpretation attempts to do. This is why we find here many German terms that I have not only tried to translate but also elucidate in their idiomatic sense. I decided, however, not to translate two key terms in Heidegger's thought, namely, *Dasein* and *Ereignis*. In and of themselves, these two terms are not untranslatable, but they are so with respect to the sense Heidegger gives them.

I have explained the untranslatable character, admitted by Heidegger himself, of the term *Ereignis*, which is no longer taken in its ordinary sense of event, but of appropriation. That term, according to (incorrect) popular etymology, comes from *eignen*; in fact, its true etymology stems from *Auge*, "eye," giving it the sense of being seen. It is the combination of these two senses that makes this term properly untranslatable.

The case of *Dasein*, a word which belongs to philosophical terminology, is markedly different. This term, which means literally "being-there," was formed to translate the Latin *existentia* and can be found in this sense in the works of German philosophers, in particular Kant and Hegel. Heidegger will give this term an entirely different sense, since for him Dasein designates the name of "the entity that we each time are ourselves" (BT, 27/7, trans. modified), that is to say, the human being. According to Heidegger, the human being is not a subject but that entity which is not indifferent to its Being, and for which Being is at issue (BT, 67/42). This is why the "literal" translation of Dasein as "being-there" [*être-là*] (proposed, among others, by the first French translators of *Being and Time*) was not approved by Heidegger, who declared in 1967, in the seminar on *Heraclitus*, to which his student and friend Eugen Fink had invited him, that with such a translation "everything that was gained as a new position in *Being and Time* is lost" (H, 126). Indeed, such a translation implies that the human being is understood as a pure existent in the traditional sense of the term, that is, as a pure, subsisting being. Dasein in its traditional sense is synonymous with *Vorhandensein*, which means the pure and simple presence-at-hand of a thing. In 1945, in a letter to Jean Beaufret, Heidegger suggested that Da-sein should be understood in the sense of "being-the-there," where "the there" would designate the unconcealment of *alētheia*. For, after the "turn," Da-sein (the way of writing the term that one finds at times in *Being and Time* then becomes constant) no longer designates the Being *of* man, the clearing that he is to himself as *lumen naturale* (BT, 171/133), but the clearing *of* Being in which man stands. It is thus in order to allow this double reading of the term Dasein that we must leave it untranslated. One can certainly consider that the decision not to translate is a failure, but nothing forbids us from considering this failure in a positive way, that is, as an attempt to bring out that which is to be thought on the basis of the German idiom itself rather than as the desire to put an obscure password into circulation.

All other difficulties of translation would deserve a detailed treatment. I have in each case tried to provide a minimum of explanations. The following remarks gather a few of the most important terms and provide a few supplementary explications. All I can hope is that the reader will hear the German idiom itself, without, however, ignoring the fact the "Being speaks everywhere and always in every language."

1) One of the most difficult translations concerns *Eigentlichkeit*, rendered most often by "authenticity" but sometimes also by "ownness" or "the proper." If the latter translation corresponds most accurately to the literal sense of the German term—the radical *eigen* means what is "own" or "proper"—to use it systematically could lead to ambiguities, for that which is proper, or "property" [*propriété*], translates the terms *Eigenschaft* ("property" in the sense of quality or attribute) and *Eigentum* ("property" in the sense of possession) rather than the term *Eigentlichkeit*, a neologism that signifies, in the strict sense, the fact of being properly (or truly) what one is. This is why I have often preferred translating this term by "authenticity," noting that it should not be taken in its strictly moral sense (see HQT, 23). The theme of "the proper" runs through Heidegger's entire work, from *Eigentlichkeit* to *Ereignis*, but in no way does this mean the perpetuation of the metaphysical privilege of the "value" of truth, for, just as untruth is more primordial than truth (BW, 132), "inauthenticity" is also more primordial than "authenticity" (see HQT, 23), and *Enteignis*, or "ex-propriation", is more primordial than *Ereignis* (see HQT, 65).

2) In German, the present in the temporal sense is designated by *Gegenwart*, literally, "being attentive to or awaiting" (*Warte*) that which "encounters" us (*gegen*); one understands then how Heidegger is able to see in it the authentic "to-come" or future (HQT, 67). The Latin *prae-sens*, on the contrary, means "being in front of", or "before", and we saw how Heidegger uses it to designate the horizonal schema of presence (HQT, 61), on the basis of which the awaiting of that which encounters us—that is, the ecstasis of the present—can take place. There is, however, another term in German that designates presence in a sense that is more ontological than temporal: *Anwesenheit*. It literally means the "coming (*an*) to Being and to its presencing," for the old verb *wesan* means "to dwell, to deploy one's being" (see HQT, 66), and the word *Anwesen*, like the Greek *ousia*, has the sense of goods or property (cf. GA 31, 51).

3) *Geworfenheit*, which designates a fundamental existentiale of Dasein, was first translated in French by a term of Latin origin, dereliction, which designates a state of abandon, when the German instead stresses the "dynamic" character of Dasein as a being that is constantly "in projection" or "in throw" (*werfen* means to throw, or to project). More recent translations of *Being and*

Time have returned to a more literal rendering of this term, "being-thrown," allowing Heidegger to relate *Geworfenheit* with that other fundamental existentiale of Dasein, *Entwurf,* projection in the sense of a first throw or sketch of possibilities (cf. BT, 185/145, and HQT, 26)

4) Like most translators, I have opted to render *Geschichtlichkeit* by *historialité* (historicality), and *geschichtlich* by *historial* (historical). Unlike the French, which has only one word to designate history, the German has two: *Geschichte,* which comes from the verb *geschehen,* meaning "to occur," "to take place," "the historical process in its reality itself" (see HQT, 44); and *Historie,* from the Greek *historia,* meaning "an inquiry," "research," "information," a term which does not refer to the historical reality itself but to the scientific knowledge of it.

5) *Sorge,* like the Latin *cura,* has the twofold sense of care and concern, and was chosen by Heidegger to designate, without any moral or existential connotation, the very being of Dasein (HQT, 27). Yet, because Dasein relates not only to itself but also to other entities, Heidegger distinguishes two modes of care: concern (*Besorgen*) and solicitude (*Fürsorge*). We saw that in concern, Dasein as being-in-the-world comports itself toward the entity that it is not by being-alongside it (HQT, 27). We were not able, however, to be as explicit concerning solicitude (which appears, though, on the schema, page 36, next to concern). Heidegger shows, in §26 of *Being and Time,* that in solicitude Dasein comports itself toward the entity that is like it, that is, the other Dasein.

I made a point of translating the terms *Zeitlichkeit* (temporality) and (its double from a Latin origin) *Temporalität* (Temporality) with the same term, distinguishing them only through the help of a capital letter (HQT, 57). It is when used as adjectives that their differences are most visible. If "Temporal" simply means that which has a relation to time, and "temporal" that which is in the mode of time, one should, on the other hand, call "intratemporal" (*innerzeitig*) what is *in* time (see HQT, 48ff).

The main difficulty of translation, which all translators have encountered, is the opposition between *Vorhandenheit* and *Zuhandenheit,* terms that both include a reference to the hand (*hand*). But if *Hand* is clearly heard by a German ear in the expression *zuhanden,* which signifies "handy" (this is why I translated *Zuhandenheit* by "handiness" [*maniabilité*]), it is not the same for *vorhanden,* which designates the pure and simple available presence of some thing. Heidegger himself stresses (BT, 67/42) that *Vorhandenheit* translates the Latin *existentia.* I have emphasized, following Heidegger (HQT, 42), the temporal, as opposed to the spatial, sense of the prefix *Vor,* which means "before" rather than "in front of." This is why I have sometimes translated *Vorhandenheit* not only by "presence-at-hand" (HQT, 60) but also by "pre-sence" (HQT, 42); and *vorhanden* not only by "present-at-hand" but also by "given beforehand" (HQT, 36), in insisting on the prior character of the available presence of things which are not yet "at hand," and therefore not for (*zu*) it.

Notes

TRANSLATORS' PREFACE

1. Françoise Dastur, *Dire le Temps* (Fougères: Editions Encre Marine, 1994), 17.
2. Françoise Dastur, *La mort* (Paris: Hatier, 1994).
3. Françoise Dastur, *Hölderlin. Tragédie et modernité* (Fougères: Editions Encre Marine, 1992).
4. *Heidegger and the Question of Time*, xxix. Hereafter all references to *Heidegger and the Question of Time* will be cited as HQT.

INTRODUCTION TO THE ENGLISH EDITION

1. Even Victor Farias mentions this point, in *Heidegger and Nazism* (Philadelphia: Temple University Press, 1989).
2. Martin Heidegger, Zürich seminar, 6 November 1951, in *Poesie*, n° 13 1980, 54.
3. Namely, Marion Heinz's excellent work, *Zeitlichkeit und Temporalität im Frühwerk Martin Heideggers* (Amsterdam: Würzburg, Königshausen und Neumann, Rodopi, 1982), which I draw substantially from and cite in my book.
4. Nietzsche, *The Twilight of the Idols*, in *The Portable Nietzsche* (New York: The Viking Press, 1954), 481.
5. BW, 204: "Metaphysics thinks of man on the basis of *animalitas* and does not think in the direction of his *humanitas*."
6. As we mentioned in our preface (HQT, x), we render *Temporal* and *Temporalität* by capitalizing the English equivalents ("Temporal" and "Temporality"). *Zeitlich* and *Zeitlichkeit* will be rendered by the same terms, in lower case [Translators].
7. One of the first articles on *Being and Time* was written by Herbert Marcuse, then a student of Heidegger—and was entitled "Contributions to a Phenomenology of Historical Materialism"—who did not hesitate to propose a *rapprochement* between Marx and Heidegger.

PRESENTATION

1. "Beingness" translates *étantité*, which itself is a translation of *Seiendheit*, or Being understood as the totality and universality of beings. Heidegger usually uses that term when referring to the *metaphysical* understanding of Being, which is oblivious of the difference between Being and beings [Translators].
2. Françoise Dastur usually puts "authentic" in quotation marks to neutralize its moral connotation. Other possible translations for *Eigentlich* and *Uneigentlich* could be "proper" and "improper," following the German distinction between *echt, unecht* ("authentic, genuine"), and *eigentlich, uneigentlich* ("proper, improper") [Translators].

CHAPTER 2:   The Temporality of Dasein and the Finitude of Time

1. We render *Befindlichkeit* by "disposition," following an indication of Heidegger himself in his 1955 lecture "What Is Philosophy," WP, 77 [Translators].
2. *Sens* has the senses both of "meaning" and of "direction"; each is present in this particular usage [Translators].

CHAPTER 3:   The Incompleteness of "Being and Time" and the Thinking of Ereignis

1. The expression *être à l'origine de* ("to be at the origin of") means to be the cause or the author of something [Translators].
2. There is a polysemy of the term *fin*: both "end" and "goal" [Translators].
3. This expression is found in §28 of Kant's *Anthropology* [Translators].
4. Dastur refers here to a translator's note in the French translation of the lecture *Die Sprache* (in *Acheminement vers la parole* [Paris; Gallimard, 1976] p. 28) [Translators].
5. The note reads in the original: "*Die Überwindung der Horizonts als solchen*" [Translators].

CHAPTER 4:   Remarks on the Translation of Key Terms

1. Some of these notes are particularly relevant for the French text, but we have generally kept them because of their philosophical significance and the light they shed on questions of translation [Translators].
2. A translation of the first division of *Being and Time* appeared in France in 1964, by R. Boehm and A. de Waelhens. In 1985, E. Martineau published an unauthorized version of the whole work (not available in bookstores), allegedly in order to protest against the delay taken by the "official" translation, which finally came out with Editions Gallimard in 1986, by François Vezin. Most readers of Heidegger in France consult the last two translations. There are vigorous polemics on the merits of each. For an instructive "comparative study" of the three translations, see Pierre Jacerme, "A propos de la traduction française de *Etre et Temps*, in "Heidegger Studies" (Berlin: Duncker & Humbolt, 1987/88, Volume 3/4), pp. 155–199. Also see in the same volume the dossier on this question, "On Reading and Translating Heidegger" [Translators].

Index

———◆———

77